PURITANISM IN SEVENTEENTH-CENTURY MASSACHUSETTS

PURITANISM IN SEVENTEENTH-CENTURY MASSACHUSETTS

Edited by DAVID D. HALL
Yale University

HOLT RINEHART AND WINSTON
New York • Chicago • San Francisco • Atlanta
Dallas • Montreal • Toronto • London

Cover illustration: A page from *History of Plimoth Plantation* written between 1630 and 1651 by William Bradford, governor of Plymouth Colony. The manuscript was stored in the Old South Church in Boston, stolen by British soldiers during the Revolution, found in the library of the Bishop of London in 1855, and returned to the United States in 1897. It is now in the State Library in Boston. (*Historical Pictures Service*)

Library of Congress Catalog Card Number: 68-16786
2559052
Printed in the United States of America
2 3 4 5 6 7 8 9

CONTENTS

Richard Mather (1596-1669), Congregational minister in Massachusetts, the original drafter of the *Cambridge Platform* (1648) which became the basic rule of New England churches. (Woodcut by John Foster, earliest known portrait engraving to have been made in America—*The Granger Collection*)

INTRODUCTION

Puritanism is the name for the way of life brought to America by the founders of Massachusetts. In the dozen years before 1640, some fifteen thousand Englishmen crossed the Atlantic in order to establish a "Holy Commonwealth" in which that way of life could flourish. Though the Holy Commonwealth lasted only a few decades, Puritanism has left a permanent mark upon American history.

Was Puritanism an influence for the good or the bad in American life? This question has provoked a major quarrel in our culture. Critics declare that the Puritans were intolerant, and cite their persecution of religious dissenters: In the 1630s the colonists banished Roger Williams, a lonely defender of freedom of conscience, and Anne Hutchinson, an Antinomian; in the 1650s, they executed three Quakers. Puritanism, say its critics, was also intellectually backward: In 1692 the colonists hanged (not burned) nineteen persons for practicing witchcraft.

Even in their own time the founders of Massachusetts were criticized for their intolerance. But by the beginning of the nineteenth century, when Puritanism was becoming only a memory, many New Englanders had come to feel that the colonists had left a valuable heritage. At the bicentenerary celebration of the Pilgrims' landing at Plymouth, Daniel Webster praised the colonists for demanding the freedom to do as they wished. Their love of freedom was the seed, Webster declared, out of which had grown the tree of American Liberty. A similar argument appears in the writings of many nineteenth-century historians. One of the more prominent was John Gorham Palfrey (1796-1881), who insisted throughout his lengthy *Compendious History of New England* that the charge of bigotry against his ancestors was not supported by the historical evidence. Palfrey seemed to make a convincing case, and by the end of the century the Puritans were generally regarded as the founders of American democracy.

Perhaps a reaction was inevitable. When it occurred, it came as a part of a broad shift in American values. In the early years of the twentieth century many artists and intellectuals began to complain that American culture was supermoralistic and anti-intellectual. According to their reading of American history, the blame for this moralism fell upon the Puritans, who now re-emerged as premature Victorians. In the 1920s, when Freudianism became popular, these critics turned to blaming the Puritans for the repressive tendencies in American life. The chief

Puritan-baiter of the period, H. L. Mencken, summed up the popular image of the colonists in his quip that Puritanism was "the haunting fear that someone, somewhere, may be happy."

Whether the Puritans were gloomy or gay is a problem that has no real connection with the questions historians now ask about them. But historians are rarely able to isolate themselves from the general values of their times, and in their interpretations of Puritanism, contemporary attitude and the historical understanding of Puritanism match each other closely.

The relationship between the two was obvious in the case of historians who insisted that Massachusetts was a "theocracy." In a generally accepted definition of a theocracy the ministers (or the churches) control the civil government. At the close of the nineteenth century, two members of a famous New England family, Brooks and Charles Francis Adams, argued that seventeenth-century Massachusetts was a theocracy in these terms. John Gorham Palfrey did not agree, but the Adamses dismissed Palfrey's interpretation because he had a "filiopietistic" bias toward New England history: He had excused or ignored the tyrannical control of the theocrats in order to cover up for his ancestors. Unlike Palfrey, the Adamses did not hide their own dislike of the Puritan system. From their point of view the central theme of Massachusetts history was the gradual emancipation of society from the authority of the ministers.

It is not surprising that the same hostility toward Puritanism colored histories of New England written during the 1920s. The two leading interpreters of Puritanism during that period, James Truslow Adams (he was not related to the other Adamses) and Vernon L. Parrington, both shaped their studies around the theme of emancipation. To this they added the new dimension of social conflict. In their view the ministers, together with laymen like John Winthrop, formed a socioeconomic elite that wanted an oligarchical form of government for reasons of class interest. The early history of Massachusetts involved not only a struggle for freedom from the thought control of the theocracy, but also a conflict between the upper and lower classes for power. Adams and Parrington thus merged the popular prejudice against Puritanism with the current appeal of class conflict.

Another question these "theocratic" historians raised about the colonists was the nature of their religious and intellectual life. Were the Puritans an early version of the Fundamentalists because they dared not depart from the authority of the Bible? According to Adams and Parrington, the answer is yes. The colonists had built their society strictly along Biblical lines. The rest of their ideas came from the *Institutes* of John Calvin. It was from Calvin that they derived their key religious principle, the absolute sovereignty of God. In turn this principle accounted for the moralism and authoritarianism that pervaded religious and social life in Massachusetts. Puritanism was a grim affair, the theocratic historians concluded, because it was narrow-minded.

This interpretation soon met with a challenge. About 1930 Adams and Parrington came under attack from a group of historians whose sympathies and scholarship led them to different conclusions about the nature of Puritanism. Sympathies changed with the temper of the times. In the aftermath of World War I and the Depression, a yearning for freedom gave way to an appreciation of man's limits, an appreciation the new age shared with the Puritans. When combined with a vast amount of new research, this change in attitude inspired a "revisionist" appraisal of the colonists. The net effect of revisionism was to reverse, once again, the popular understanding of the Puritans. Since the 1930s, the revisionist interpretation has become the new orthodoxy.

The two historians most responsible for the new interpretation were Samuel Eliot Morison and Perry Miller. Out of their research came the conclusion that, far from being anti-intellectual, the Puritans sustained a complex and humanistic intellectual life. As for their attitude toward moral behavior, Morison and Miller deny that the colonists were kill-joys and criticize Mencken for confounding Puritanism with Victorianism.

Because the revisionists freed themselves from the old prejudice against the Puritans, they were able to appreciate the spiritual vigor at the heart of the movement. The theocratic historians had painted the colonists in drab colors to match the supposedly fatalistic doctrine of predestination. The Puritan way of life, as they conceive it, was a joyless routine of obeying the commands of a harsh and distant God. In the writings of Perry Miller, from which the first selection is taken, a different picture emerges. Miller argues that the New England Puritans believed in a modified Calvinism, or "covenant theology," that allowed for man's activity in the process of salvation. Puritanism was not fatalistic, therefore, but a stimulus to action. In the Puritan's spiritual life, concludes Miller, there was an "exhilaration of faith" that made existence profoundly exciting.

Samuel Eliot Morison, the other leading revisionist, challenges the notion that the Puritans were intellectually backward. In the second selection he brings together a wide variety of evidence to indicate the breadth and generosity of the colonists' intellectual life. Calvin was not the only author they read; works of St. Thomas Acquinas and many other non-Puritans were also to be found on their bookshelves. Puritanism, argue Morison and Miller, was a synthesis of Renaissance humanism and Calvinistic piety.

If Puritanism was a blend of piety and intellect, the balance, as the revisionists assess it, seems to be in favor of the intellectual heritage. In the third selection Alan Simpson corrects this emphasis. He insists that the peculiar mark of the Puritan movement was its conception of the spiritual life, specifically the conversion experience that Puritans assumed to be normative.

All interpreters of Puritanism agree that the colonists' religious ideas played an important role in shaping the development of Massachusetts. Whether the Puritans were narrow-minded Calvinists or Elizabethan Englishmen is a question that leads directly to the central problem about the Holy Commonwealth. Was it an authoritarian society run by an upper class elite? Did the ministers, as members of this elite, control the government? What social and political ideas did they share with statesmen like John Winthrop, the first governor of the colony?

Different answers to the first of these questions appear in the assessments of Winthrop by James Truslow Adams and Edmund S. Morgan. Winthrop was undoubtedly the most powerful figure in Massachusetts during the early years of the colony. In 1630, when he arrived as governor, he brought with him the charter that Charles I had granted to the Massachusetts Bay Company. According to the charter, authority to govern the *company* was vested in the stockholders, or "freemen," who elected officers to carry on the day-by-day affairs. Winthrop faced the task of adjusting this form of government to suit the needs of the *colony*. The first important modification, made in the fall of 1630, was to extend the rights of freemanship to persons who were not stockholders in the company. Subsequently, in the spring of 1631, a law was passed providing that only church members were eligible to become freemen.

Did Winthrop make the first of these changes deliberately, or was he forced by popular pressure to loosen his control? Was the law of 1631 a device by which the theocrats could stay in power? Certainly Winthrop was no democrat if that term implies a belief in human equality: He said that "God Almighty, in his most holy and wise providence, hath so disposed of the condition of mankind as in all times some must be. . .high and eminent in power and dignity, others mean and in subjection." But did he want to exclude the mass of the people from sharing in the government? Morgan, the revisionist historian, takes issue with Adams' account of Winthrop's motives and insists that within Puritanism itself Winthrop found reasons for enlarging the access to power. And Morgan argues that the law of 1631 did not function as a barrier to political democracy.

Winthrop and John Cotton, the leading minister in Massachusetts, expressed similar ideas about the nature of government. Cotton was opposed to "democracy," as Vernon L. Parrington points out, but the question raised by B. Katherine Brown concerns the meaning of this term as Cotton used it. Reviewing many of the same passages from Cotton's writing that Parrington cites, Mrs. Brown finds, as does Morgan, that the political theory of the Puritans admitted the people into the structure of government. Do her definitions of the terms democracy and aristocracy help to account for the change made in 1630?

In Parrington's sketch of John Cotton appears another theme of the theocratic historians, that the Holy Commonwealth was a religious utopia based on rules laid down in the Bible. One way of testing this theory is to determine the source (or sources) of the colony's law codes. John Cotton was one of the persons who drafted the first set of laws, and according to Parrington, he took his ideas directly from the Bible. But George L. Haskins reached a different conclusion after examining the sources of the law code of 1648. The colonists, he suggests, were faithful to certain traditions of English law even in the way they observed the Bible.

Around the figure of John Cotton revolves another of the questions in dispute, the relationship between church and state. Brooks Adams, one of the first to argue the theocratic interpretation, states the case flatly: The ministers were the real power in Massachusetts and bent the civil magistrates to their will. But Aaron B. Seidman presents evidence to show that the colonists believed in the separation of church and state, and restricted the powers of both in order to keep them equal. Could these restrictions prevent the ministers from exercising the authority Adams claims they had? He and Seidman also dispute the meaning of the law of 1631 that required church membership of prospective voters. Was this law simply a way for the ministers to gain political power?

All of the discussion so far has covered only the first twenty years (1630-1650) of the history of Massachusetts. About the middle of the century the founders of the Holy Commonwealth began to complain of "declension," a word that referred to a declining zeal for purity. It was not only the inner spirit of the colonists that was changing; the laws and political structure of the colony were also affected. After the restoration of Charles II to the English throne, the Crown began to assert its authority over Massachusetts. Soon the colony was forced to practice religious toleration, and eventually, in 1692, it had to accept a royal governor. These changes meant the end of the society that Winthrop and Cotton had originally envisaged.

Long before the end of the seventeenth century many colonists had broken away from the orthodox patterns of belief and behavior. Conflicts in the churches, in the towns, and even among the leaders of the colony were part of its history from the very beginning. These conflicts offer important clues to the role of certain groups or of certain ideas in bringing about social change. And because they reveal complex patterns of practice and belief, these conflicts cast doubt upon any monolithic interpretation of New England Puritanism.

In the 1630s merchants in Boston quarreled with the leaders of Massachusetts over the enforcement of the Puritans' business ethic. As described by Bernard Bailyn, this ethic was aimed at controlling certain forms of economic activity which the merchants felt they should carry on freely. Their disagreement over economic policy came into the open in the case of Robert Keayne. What was Keayne's reaction to his trial? What role would the merchant class play in changing the structure of Massachusetts society?

In the meantime the churches were debating whether to change their standards of church membership. Herbert W. Schneider argues that the second generation of colonists no longer felt the same sense of sin as the first, and for this reason agreed to a relaxation of the standards. But Morgan proposes another interpretation of the key step in this decline, the so-called "Half-Way Covenant." Starting from a description of the original tests for church membership—tests that were unusually strict even for Puritans—he points out that later generations had to face certain inevitable problems. What "basic responsibility" came into conflict with the original quest for "purity"? Would a renewed awareness of this responsibility explain the Half-Way Covenant?

In the final essay Darrett B. Rutman questions many assumptions about New England Puritanism. His quarrel is as much with the revisionists as with the theocratic historians; but his conclusions clearly align him on the side of those who reject the conception of a theocratic, closed society. What made the ideas of Winthrop ineffective in the situations Rutman describes? What light does his evidence throw upon the relationship between church and state? A deeper question than these, and one that historians like Rutman are just beginning to face, is the relationship between ideology and institutions in the early history of Massachusetts.

In the reprinted selections footnotes appearing in the original sources have in general been omitted unless they contribute to the argument or better understanding of the selection.

The person most responsible for the current revival of interest in the Puritans is PERRY MILLER (1905-1963), who spent his entire career as a scholar at Harvard and wrote a massive synthesis of *The New England Mind.* He began his investigation of Puritanism in the early 1930s, at a time when Puritanism was considered merely an appendage of Calvinism and Calvinism meant a "hellfire and brimstone" approach to the spiritual life. Immersing himself in the original sources, Miller emerged with a fresh understanding of Puritan religious ideas, particularly of the rational, voluntaristic elements in Puritan theology. Miller had a remarkable capacity to identify with his subject. Because he seemed to speak so clearly from within the Puritan movement, his interpretation has been widely accepted by later scholars. °

Puritan Spirituality and Predestination

The historian of the New England Puritans frequently has occasion to lament the many dry bones of metaphysics and abstruse theology which he is compelled to turn up in the effort to resurrect a semblance of that extinct species; his construction is bound all too often to resemble one of those grinning skeletons of antediluvian monsters, imperfectly wired together and stored in some museum of paleontology, making altogether too exorbitant a demand upon the imagination of the spectator to carry the conviction that the creature ever lived and breathed and moved. The vast differences between the intellect of the seventeenth century and the present necessitate so much laborious restatement of the abstractions of Puritanism that the flesh and blood realities of the Puritans themselves are lost to view. It is supremely difficult for us to imagine that the doctrine was not always present in their minds as we find it embalmed in a crabbed catechism, and still more difficult for us to understand that to them it was an all pervading sensibility, a depth of feeling, and a way of life, that it was not only of the mind but just as much of the heart and the passions.

When we come to examine the sermons, the words delivered from the pulpits by living men to living ears, we find that the

°Reprinted from *The Puritans*, edited by Perry Miller and Thomas H. Johnson (New York: Harper & Row, Publishers, 1938), pp. 281-289. Footnotes omitted. Copyright 1938, 1966 by Thomas H. Johnson and the Estate of Perry Miller.

ideas therein discussed were indeed those of the creed, the dogmas of original sin, irresistible grace, and predestination. But they were not developed as points in a formal lecture, or expounded as curious and technical problems; they were not preached as doctrines, or contentions, or theories, but as vivid facts. The systematized theology served primarily as a frame of reference within which the issues of human existence could be confronted immediately. The language employed was not that of the schoolroom and the textbook, but of the streets, of trades, of adventures. The sentences were not bare abstractions, but concrete dramatizations, replete with the imagery of fishing, farming, carpentering, of the city and the meadow, of the seasons and of the moods of men. The method of developing sermons from texts in the Bible strengthened this tendency to concrete and solid presentation; the ministers did not select a doctrine to preach upon, and then hunt texts to support it, but they took this or that text and deciphered its meaning. That man is naturally bound in sin and must hang upon the dispensations of grace from God—this was a dogma; but as Thomas Hooker preaches, it takes form no longer as a colorless generalization, but as an unforgettable picture:

> You know the Dog must stay till his Master comes in, and when hee is come, hee must stay till he sit downe, and till hee cut his meate, and hee must not have the meate from his trencher neither, when he hath stayed all this while, he hath nothing but the crums. So it is with a poore sinner; you must not thinke that God will bee at your becke: No, you must bee content with the crums of mercy, and pity, and lye under the table til the Lord let the crums fall.

That a regenerate man progresses from the initial stage of illumination to a fuller and deeper immersion in grace was a tenet of the creed; but as John Cotton develops it. . .through the metaphor of a man wading into the waters of a shallow beach and at last reaching the cool depths, out of sight of land, the paragraph, instead of being a logical proof, becomes an ecstatic prose poem.

The most persistent misunderstanding of the Puritan mind in contemporary criticism results in the charge that it was fatalistic. To one unfamiliar with the inward power of the belief, who judges merely upon the external evidence of the doctrine, there seems no conceivable motive for positive human exertion; the logical inference from the decrees of predestination and reprobation would seem to be the. . . frame of mind in which a man says, "God does not send me grace, I can't convert myself," and gives over trying. Though the Puritan did indeed live much of his life by logic, he did not so live all of it or even the most important part of it. Dialectics and syllogisms do not account for the driving force of the Massachusetts settlers, or for the vehemence of the Ironsides' cavalry charges, whose enemies "God made as stubble to our swords." . . .Perhaps the finest statement of the invigorating effects of a philosophy of divine determination is Oliver Cromwell's account of his thoughts before the battle of Naseby, when his ranks of "poor, ignorant men" were being drawn up to face the oncoming host of gallant and flashing cavaliers; then, says Cromwell, "I could not, riding alone about my business, but smile out to God in praises, in assurance of victory, because God would, by things that are not, bring to naught things that are. Of which I had great assurance, and God did it." How men could work themselves into this frame of mind, combining trust in God's disposing power with an assurance of victory, going through fire and water in order that what was decreed might be fulfilled, what sort of thinking brought them to this conclusion, may appear by. . .the sermons of Thomas Hooker. His exhaustive analysis of the true sight of sin, and his stirring account of the struggle of the saint with inherent evil uncover the sources of that almost titanic energy of which the Puritans were so abundantly possessed. A true sight of sin, he says, consists in perceiving it "clearly" and "convictingly," and the imagery by which he brings home the full brilliance of the clarity and the overwhelming weight of the conviction makes clear why there was little need for him to dwell upon a remote and semi-mythological fall of Adam, or no need whatsoever to entangle his auditors in the subtleties of free will, foreordination and absolute decree. Anyone who ever saw himself as pitilessly as Hooker requires would thereafter spend his days and nights in feverish exertions to lift himself out of such a mire of depravity. When the soul saw its task, thus clearly and convictingly, as a fact, not a theory, then also the need for divine assistance in escaping the clutch of sin was no longer something to be proved by a series of geometrical corollaries but became a desperate hunger gnawing ceaselessly at a man's very vitals. The thrill, the excitement, the challenge of the conflict against Satan would entirely drive out of his mind the suggestion that he might better fold his hands and await the pleasure of God. When we consider how intense, in Puritan eyes, was the warfare of the spirit and the flesh, and how interminable a campaign the true soldier of Christ undertook when he enrolled himself in the regiment of the godly, then we can perhaps gauge the true sublimity of Puritanism as we find Hooker insisting, and his congregation no doubt agreeing, that the awakened sinner should actually be grateful to the minister who by his winged sermons had pierced the doors of his complacency, he should be overjoyed that he had been dragged against all his natural inclinations from the peace and security of a false contentment into the heat and fury of this battle.

Inspired volunteers, going forth under the banners of truth, do not make lazy or halfhearted campaigners. But if the religion of the Puritan was intense, it was not foolhardy. He was ecstatic, but not insane. He employed self-analysis, meditation, and incessant soul-searching to drive out sin from one stronghold after another; in every siege he had to be not only valiant, but self-controlled, patient, wary, and crafty. It was an entirely subjective struggle; the victories were gained within the soul, and the final triumph could never be won on this side of the grave. Consequently while the saints were occupied internally with the conquest of evil, they could not expect to fare externally any better than others. All men must live among men and as men; whether their souls are filled with the Holy Ghost or not, they must suffer the diseases and decays to which men are subject. The exhilaration of faith is known to the heart of the believer, but as Samuel Willard explains, those inward supports are remote from public view. Appearances therefore are deceiving, and the saint must keep his wits about him; he must remain calm in the midst of ardor, he must burn with fervor, but always be detached and analytical, to make sure that his agitation is genuinely of the spirit, not of mere human cupidity, and to guard against suffocating the flame with false assurances and outward conformity. Puritanism would make every man an expert psychologist, to detect all makeshift "rationalizations," to shatter without pity the sweet dreams of self-enhancement in which the ego takes refuge from reality. A large quantity of Puritan sermons were devoted to exquisite analyses of the differences between "hypocrites" and saints, and between one kind of hypocrite and another, to exposing not merely the conscious duplicity of evil men, but the abysmal tricks which the subconscious can play upon the best of men. The duty of the Puritan in this world was to know himself—without sparing himself one bit, without flattering himself in the slightest, without concealing from himself a single unpleasant fact about himself.

In the course of this sustained and unmitigated meditation, he perpetually measured himself by the highest imaginable excellency. The Puritan was taught to approve of no act because it was good enough for the circumstances, to rest content with no performance because it was the best that could be done in this or that situation. He knew indeed that life is imperfect, that the purest saints do not ever entirely disentangle themselves from the meshes of corruption, but though perfection was unattainable—even more because it was so—he bent every nerve and sinew to attempting the attainment. The Puritan life might be compared to that of a poet laboring under penalty of death to produce several hundred lines a day, and yet driven by an acute critical sense to despise every passage, every phrase that did not flow from the fountain of fresh and original inspiration. Nothing was to be done by the force of habit, in the facility of mere technical proficiency, by mechanical routine; ideally every moment and every action should reveal radiations of the supernal vitality. So far as men fell short of this ideal, they were contemptible. Over against this transcendent standard, physical existence was inevitably seen as frail, transitory, and unprofitable. When two Harvard students broke through the ice while skating, and were drowned, Increase Mather drew the moral that the times of men are in the hand of God, that no one knows when the blow will fall upon himself, or what lies in wait for him tomorrow or the day after. No trust is to be put in the things of this world, no reliance placed upon material devices. Life is a chronicle of accidents and blunders, reversals and hopes defeated.

But at the same time, if life in the world is a melancholy spectacle, it is not a tale told by an idiot; there is indeed sound and fury, but behind the meaningless futility of appearances there stand the ranks of the eternal verities. The ax-head may slip, as Urian Oakes says, and the skull of an innocent and good man be split; but the Puritan is not thereupon to cry, "Out, out—." The blade was guided by the steady hand of God, and somewhere, somehow there is a reason for this casualty, there must be a justice behind the apparent injustice. Men may not readily see it;. . .they may be hard pressed to explain why some events turn out as they do, and be brought time and time again to confess that in this or that series of misfortunes or streaks of luck they can not discover the wisdom of God. Nevertheless, that He who orders all things does order them by the counsel of His perfect reason and that nothing in the world is really chance, accident, or blind fate—this was the constant and unshakable conviction of the Puritan. The one thing he insisted upon, however, was that in order that this conviction might be upheld, no realities should be glossed over, no horror and no agony denied. The assertion was to be made with a clear-eyed perception of things as they do fall out, for weal or for woe.

All events therefore have their reason and their logic. We must train to the full extent of our capacities to discover the reason and comprehend the logic. But our finite minds can not grasp all things, and our corrupted intellects can not understand all the things we grasp. No matter how much we know, there will always remain a margin to the page of knowledge which we cannot explore; the limits of the universe are not searchable with the human eye. The labor demanded of the intelligent man is that he give over no exertion to account for things, that he never accept without endeavouring to explain, that he never take a conclusion on trust until he has exhausted all means to take it on reason; but all the time he must remember that explanation can only go so far, that mortal reason is not God's reason, that there is always more ignorance to be confessed than certain knowledge to be enjoyed. The Puritan was completely hospitable to the revolutionizing discoveries made by physical science during the seventeenth century, but as long as he remained true to the fundamentals of Puritanism he was not deceived into concluding that man had at last unriddled the universe.

What the admirable sagacity of future ages may compass as to thousands of problems within the circle of Sciences, or in that most noble Art of Chymistry, or the Analysis of the three kingdoms of nature: the tubes and glasses of our present inventions give us no sufficient prospect. . . . The learned of this age wonder at the denial of the motion of the Earth, tho now the truth of it appears clear to all of the generality of the ingenious of *Europe*. . .

Indeed so may posterity deride at these our ages, and the more ingenious of future times, may stand amazed at our dulness and stupidity about minerals, meteors and the cure of diseases, and many thousand things besides, about the lustre of stars and precious stones, which may be as easy to them as letters to us. . .Such rare inventions may be given in of God to beautifie the glory of the latter days. All our writings in Divinity, will be like insipid water, to what shall then appear upon the Stage,. . .and the Artists that shall then be born, may discover more things in the works of God to be discust and endeavoured to be explained, then they themselves shall arrive to. The superfine Wisdom and Learned Wits of those acute times will discover vast regions of darkness and ignorance. There will be a *plus ultra* to the end of the world. . .if in millions of things we are stunted and fooled at every turn, that we may cry out with the Satyrist—*Auriculas Asini quis non habet?* What fearful sots are we in the things before us? Then what shall dull reason do in the great sublimities and solemnities of faith, and the doctrine set forth by Infinite Wisdom.

It was in the eighteenth century, along with their reaction against the religious theory of society, that New Englanders abandoned the caution inculcated by this passage, and then many of them jumped as blithely as did the rest of the learned world to the comfortable conclusion that Sir Isaac Newton had explained the mind of God. Two hundred years afterwards physics has become more metaphysical than scholasticism itself, astronomers turn to writing "in Divinity," and before our superfine wisdoms loom vast regions of darkness and ignorance, as the visible universe has become once again relative to itself and full of exceedingly deceptive appearances.

Urian Oakes concludes a sermon on providence with an injunction which was constantly delivered from New England pulpits: "labour to be prepared and provided for Disappointments." Put beside this another instruction which was equally recurrent through the sermons of Puritan ministers: "as the things and objects are, great, or mean, that men converse withall; so they are high or low spirited." Take these two rules together—on the one hand, to expect nothing but disappointment in this life, on the other, to cultivate a high-spirited frame of mind by converse with the highest objects of contemplation, and between these two poles the daily life of the Puritans oscillated.

John Cotton gives instructions to artisans, farmers, and merchants for the prosecution of their callings, explaining that men should pursue their worldly vocations, but not expect too much from them, should work in them, and yet labor in faith. His requirements would seem full of inconsistencies and impossibilities to one unadjusted to the dual contention of the Puritan synthesis: the fallibility of material existence and the infallibility of the spiritual, the necessity for living in a world of time and space according to the laws of that time and that place, with never once forgetting that the world will pass, be resolved back into nothingness, that reality and permanence belong to things not as they appear to the eye but to the mind.

It is by the Spiritual Operations and Actions of our minds that we meet with the Lord, and have a kind of intercourse with the Almighty, who is a Spirit. For al outward things are for the body, the body for the soul, the soul is nextly for God, and therefore meets as really with him in the Actions of Understanding, as the Eye meets with the Light in Seeing; which no other Creature can do, nor no action of a bodily Creature doth. Our Sences in their sinful and inordinate swervings, when they become means and in-lets of evil from their objects, they meet with the Creature firstly, and there make the jar: It's the beauty of the Object that stirs up to lust by the Eye, the daintiness of the Diet that provokes to intemperance by the tast, the harsh and unkind language that provokes to wrath and impatience by the Ear: But the Mind and Understanding toucheth the Lord directly, meets with his Rule, and with God acting in the way of his Government there, and when it goes off from the Rule as before, and attends its own vanity and folly, it justles with the Almighty, stands in open defyance and resistance against him.

The man who is misled by appearances "justles" with God, and is not merely a sinner and a reprobate; he is, still more tragically, a man to whom reality, the order of things "as they be," will never become known. Puritanism was regulated by the possibility of each man's achieving this insight, on whatever level of culture or education he dwelt, with the aid of divine grace; the assumption was that once this comprehension was gained, men would be able to live amid disappointments without being disappointed, amid deceptions without being deceived, amid temptations without yielding to them, amid cruelties without becoming cruel.

The ideal of conduct thus held out was definitely affirmative. There is very little preaching of hell-fire in seventeenth-century sermons; Hooker's sentences are as far in that direction as any minister went before the beginning of the evangelical revival and the thunderings of Jonathan Edwards. So often are the first Puritans accused of living in fear and trembling under the threat of eternal torment that this point needs to be heavily underscored. That the ministers did not play upon their congregations' nerves by painting the horrors of the pit was because, for one thing no doubt, the sensibilities of people in the seventeenth century were inured to violence. This was still the age in which mothers took their children for a treat to public executions. In part the lack of brimstone sermons is accounted for by the Puritan disinclination to make religion emotional at the cost of judicious analysis and sound intellectual conviction. In converting sinners, said Samuel Willard, we must "imitate God"; we must "first deal with their understandings; to raise the affections, without informing the mind, is a fruitlesse unprofitable labour, and serves but to make zeal without knowledge." But still more fundamentally, Puritan ministers did not bludgeon their people with the bloody club of damnation because their eyes were fixed upon the positive side of religion, upon the beauties of salvation, the glory of God, and the joy of faith. The worst they could imagine for the reprobate was not physical burnings and unslaked thirst, but the deprivation of God's spirit.

> There is a great deal goes to the eternal life of a soul, and thou hast none of it; thou wantest the love of God, which is better than life; thou wantest grace which is indeed the inward principle of life in the soul; thou wantest the promise which is the support of the soul here in this life.

What were racks and tortures compared to the want of these things? The applications or "uses" of all doctrines stated in the sermons stress continually the note of hope, the possibility that anyone, no matter how immoral or depraved he has been, may yet be saved; it is only with the next century that men are bluntly told how God abhors them and holds them over the pit of Hell as one holds a spider or some loathsome insect over the fire. When the seventeenth-century preacher wanted to arouse men he would tell them not of the irreversible sentence passed upon them in the future world, but would instance afflictions already suffered, or predict those to come, in this world—plagues, fires, earthquakes, and shipwrecks—punishments that men might survive and from which they might profit. This tendency undoubtedly produced some unpleasant characteristics, and gave opportunity for such an egotist as Increase Mather, or for such an egomaniac as his son Cotton, to hurl the vengeance of God at persons or actions they themselves did not happen to like, and even forced solid minds like John Winthrop's to twist coincidences into special interpositions of the deity. The bent of the seventeenth-century Puritan was to portray God as indeed a stern disciplinarian and one not to be trifled with, but nevertheless not as a savage chief exulting in the protracted writhings of his helpless captives. The deity was first and foremost the source of that spirit of peace to which some men might attain, "and sometimes in that unspeakable measure, as that it passeth the understanding of a man to conceive." Not all men would or could reach this light, but no single individual need ever give over the hope that he might discover himself one of the favored, or ever abandon the endeavor to make himself one of them.

Starting about 1930 SAMUEL ELIOT MORISON (1887-), for many years professor of American history at Harvard and author of a three-volume history of the college, launched an attack upon the theocratic interpretation. Instinctively sympathetic to the Puritans, Morison discovered in the course of his research that the founders of Massachusetts were intellectually more humane and tolerant than the theocratic historians have acknowledged. He summarizes his findings in the opening chapter of *The Intellectual Life of Colonial New England*. His most significant conclusion is that the Puritans tried to sustain a high level of culture in the American wilderness. They wanted to purify the church, but they also established Harvard College to carry on the Renaissance tradition of learning.[*]

Puritanism and the Life of the Mind

In this book I propose to describe, so far as time permits, and in describing to comment on, the intellectual life of New England in the seventeenth century. It might equally be called a course on the intellectual implications of English puritanism, for in that century there was not room for much in New England outside the stimulating if restrictive embrace of puritanism. There are, to be sure, a few exceptions. William Morrell's poem on New England in Latin hexameters was (like George Sandys' translation of Ovid's *Metamorphoses*) the work of an Englishman who made a brief sojourn in America. Thomas Morton's bibulous circle at Merrymount produced some bawdy verse, a good drinking song, and an amusing tract against the puritans which entered into our literary tradition, inspiring a bad novel of the nineteenth century and a worse opera of the twentieth. Yet it was but a gay episode, in no way affecting the life or mind of the people. The descriptions of New England by nonpuritans like Captain John Smith and John Josselyn belong to English rather than American literature. New England was not only puritan, but a fair test of what values there were in English puritanism: for in New England the puritans had it pretty much their own way. The colonies that they founded were their own colonies, from which anyone who objected violently or

[*] Reprinted from Samuel Eliot Morison, *The Intellectual Life of Colonial New England* (New York: New York University Press, 1956), chap. 1. Some footnotes omitted.

even vociferously to the puritan way of life was forthwith expelled. The English government let them almost completely alone, excepting for the short-lived experiment of the Dominion of New England at the close of the century.

All the contents of this book are, in a sense, a test of English puritanism. The colonists in New England (and, for that matter, in Virginia or Canada) were severely handicapped in their struggle to keep up civilized standards. For the most part they were leading a tough pioneer life; their audience was small; their contacts with the centers of learning and culture in Europe were tenuous; their chances of publication were slight. But the puritans of New England did have it their own way as to the shape, the form, and the content of their intellectual life. Their tastes, desires, and prejudices dictated what would be read, studied, written, and published. Everyone knows that those tastes were in a sense narrow—for instance, they proscribed the drama. What is not sufficiently known or appreciated is this: puritanism not only did not prevent, but stimulated an interest in the classics, belles-lettres, poetry, and scientific research. Neither pioneer hardships nor other restrictions were ever so great as to prevent the burgeoning of a genuine intellectual life in that series of little beachheads on the edge of the wilderness, which was seventeenth-century New England.

By intellectual life I do not mean literature alone. Products of the printing press naturally bulk large among the palpable intellectual remains of any modern era; and, as historians (or some of them) dislike speculation about things impalpable, they are easily tempted to confine their attention to printed literature, or even to a few typical writers. My purpose is to depict the life of puritan New England in aspects other than its economic and political. But within so brief a compass I cannot touch architecture, or the minor arts that the early New Englanders cultivated to good purpose.

Purposely I have completely neglected in this book the works of New England's founders who were educated in old England, and who passed an appreciable part of their lives in the Old Country before emigrating. Some of these men—William Bradford, John Cotton, John Wilson, Thomas Shepard, Thomas Hooker, and Roger Williams—wrote prose superior by any standard to that of the later, native-born writers. And for that very reason, they are the much better known and far more has been written about them. My intention is, first, to describe the institutions (school and college) and facilities (libraries, printing, and bookselling) that fostered intellectual life, and then to describe what the native-born, or American-educated, New Englanders made of these opportunities.

Most writers have emphasized the institutional and material aspects of New England colonial history. This is natural, since the institutions the puritans founded, Church, Commonwealth, Town, College, were so firmly established as to outlast the purposes for which they were intended. Church and College and Commonwealth have been patched and altered again and again, without losing all their original character—much as an old mansion of New York City is cut up into flats and offices, yet retains somewhat of its original dignity. Others have confined their attention to the material side of colonial New England: farming, fishing, shipping, trading. All these activities in a sense fed the intellectual life just as modern finance and industry feed medical research, scholarship, and other objects of social value. It is not, however, my purpose to describe the old bottles that were ultimately to be filled with new wine, or the sources of wealth which paid for the wine. Rather do I seek the flavor of the old wine for which the bottles were originally blown. For the wine of New England is not a series of successive vintages, each distinct from the other, like the wines of France; it is more like the mother-wine in those great casks of port and sherry that one sees in the *bodegas* of Portugal and Spain, from which a certain amount is drawn off every year, and replaced by an equal volume of the new. Thus the change is gradual, and the mother-wine of 1656 still gives bouquet and flavor to what is drawn in 1956.

Our vintners have been a pretty close corporation. New blood and wine they have sought and obtained as the price of survival; but it is they—this hierarchy of parsons, professors, and artists—who have determined what should be selected and what rejected. The newcomers who began to arrive in appreciable numbers over a century ago, and who now rule all the cities and most of the public institutions of New England, have contributed very little to the main currents of New England intellectual life, although they manage to make some native intellectuals very unhappy. Our imported ideas have come from England, France, and Germany, rather than from the nations of our immigrant peoples.

New England differed from the other English colonies in that it was founded largely for the purpose of trying an experiment in Christian living. This statement is self-evident to anyone who has read extensively in the literature of the times, both puritan writings and writings of their enemies. It has, of course, been challenged by people so superior in intellect that they can give you the essence of an era without the labor of reading the sources. We have all been told that the dynamic motive of settling New England was economic, though expressed in a religious jargon. Doubtless the idea of bettering their condition in life was present in a very large number of early New Englanders: the spirit of adventure must also claim a share; but no one who has delved deeply into the origin and history of the New England colonies can, by any fair application of the rules of evidence, deny that the dynamic force in settling New England was English puritanism desiring to realize itself. The leaders, whom the people followed, proposed like Milton to make over a portion of the earth in the spirit of Christian philosophy: a new church and state, family and school, ethic and conduct. They might and did differ among themselves as to the realization of these high and holy aims; but a new City of God was their aim.

Until 1630, New England was anybody's country; the little band of Pilgrims who landed at Plymouth Rock ten years earlier were too few and isolated to have leavened any large lump of people hostile or indifferent to their point of view. But once the Massachusetts Bay Colony was founded, the fate of New England was sealed. In ten years' time, fifteen or twenty thousand people came over under puritan leaders; and three new colonies, Connecticut, Rhode Island, and New Haven, had been founded to contest with Massachusetts Bay in rivalry for divine favor and godly living.

Who were these puritans, and what did they propose to do? They were a party in the Church of England that arose in Elizabeth's reign with the purpose of carrying out the Protestant reformation to its logical conclusion, to base the English Church both in doctrine and discipline on the firm foundation of Sacred Scripture; or in the words of Cartwright, to restore the primitive, apostolic church 'pure and unspotted' by human accretions or inventions. Religion should permeate every phase of living. Man belonged to God alone: his only purpose in life was to enhance God's glory and do God's will, and every variety of human activity, every sort of human conduct, presumably unpleasing to God, must be discouraged if not suppressed.

English puritanism, though essentially a religious movement, had its political and economic aspects. In their search for the original pattern of the Christian church in the apostolic age, the puritan leaders did not agree. They were divided into the Presbyterians, who thought that the primitive church was governed by a series of representative assemblies or synods; and the Congregationalists, who insisted that there never had been a unified church, only churches: each individual congregation should be a democracy of the 'visible saints,' of those admitted to full communion upon satisfactory evidence that they were God's elect. New England was founded by Congregationalists, the more democratic wing; and the latent democratic principle in their polity proved, humorously enough, an exceptionally heavy cross for the autocratically inclined parsons to carry. But whether Congregational or Presbyterian in its polity, puritanism appealed to the average Englishman's anticlericalism. It gave the layman a larger part in the local church than he had enjoyed since the Roman emperors became Christian.

Puritanism also had its economic side. I do not hold to the thesis of Max Weber and Troeltsch, that puritanism arose as a justification for usury; *i.e.*, for taking interest on loans. In New England, certainly, the Church was no respecter of persons, and the spectacle of Robert Keayne, the profiteering merchant of Boston, having to stand up in meeting and take a tongue-lashing from the Reverend John Cotton for infringing the puritan code of business ethics, would have warmed the heart of any modern radical. The Weber thesis, as restated by R. H. Tawney, accords better with the facts as observed in New England. Puritanism was unascetic; it came to terms with this world. Under the medieval church you could only approach perfection (short of Heaven) by withdrawing from this world and entering the priesthood or a monastic order. But puritanism taught that a man could serve God as effectively in his chosen calling as by entering the sacred ministry; that a farmer or merchant who conducted his business according to Christian ethics was more agreeable in the sight of God than one who withdrew from the world and escaped his social responsibilities by a celibate or monastic life. This doctrine of the calling, that you could serve God by nobly fulfilling a function determined by the conditions of this world, and thus prove your right to an easy place in the next world, was probably the main reason why puritanism appealed to the rising middle class, the nascent capitalists of the sixteenth and seventeenth centuries. Puritanism was essentially a middle-class movement. It was far too exigent in its moral demands ever to be popular with earthy-minded peasants, or with the nobility and the very rich, who saw no point in having money if you could not spend it as you liked.

In its attitude toward love, puritanism had more in common with Judaism than with medieval Christianity or Jesuit piety. Puritanism did not hold with asceticism or celibacy. The clergy married young and often; their church offered no monastic retreat for men who were too much troubled by women. Milton's invocation 'Hail, wedded love!' in *Paradise Lost* expresses the puritan ideal very neatly; and William Ames, the puritan casuist, implies in his *de Conscientia* that women have a right to expect something more from their husbands than mere duty. 'Increase and multiply,' the oldest of God's commands, was one that the puritans particularly enjoyed obeying—or some of us would not be here. Continence was a moral ideal on which due weight was laid; abstinence was not a superior virtue confounded with chastity but was in conflict with the purpose of creation. Married men who came out to New England were bluntly told to send for their wives or return to them. It was easier to obtain a divorce in New England in the seventeenth century than in old England; for the puritans, having laid such store on wedded love, wished every marriage to be a success.

On its intellectual side, which mainly concerns us, puritanism was an enemy to that genial glorification of the natural man with all his instincts and appetites that characterized the Renaissance and the great Elizabethans. Shakespeare's

> What a piece of work is man! how noble in reason! how infinite in faculties! in form and moving how express and admirable! in action how like an angel! in apprehension how like a god!

is the antithesis of puritanism, which taught that natural man was wholly vile, corrupt, and prone to evil; that he could do no good without God's assistance; that he thoroughly deserved to broil in hell for all eternity, and would do so if he did not grasp the hand of grace proffered him by a merciful God through Jesus Christ.

Predestination, one of the cardinal doctrines of Calvinism, was not stressed by the New England puritans; Michael Wigglesworth does indeed touch on it when he consigns the *reprobate* infants (not the *unbaptized* infants as is commonly said) to the 'easiest room in hell'; but after reading some hundreds of puritan sermons, English and New English, I feel qualified to deny that the New England puritans were predestinarian Calvinists. John Cotton indeed was wont to 'sweeten his mouth with a bit of Calvin' before retiring (rather a sour bedtime confection, one would think), but in general the New England puritans quoted their revered Ames and Perkins and the church fathers much more than they did Calvin; and John Harvard had more volumes in his library by St. Thomas Aquinas than by St. John of Geneva. The puritan sermons assume (when they do not directly teach) that by virtue of the Covenant of Grace, and through the efforts of the churches, salvation lay within reach of every person who made an effort; Christ helped those who helped themselves.[1] Fatalism is completely wanting in the New England view of religion or of life. The karma of Buddhism implied a blind, meaningless universe; a poor joke that God played on humanity in one of his idle or sardonic humors. But the puritans, like the Jews, regarded this earth and humanity as a divine enterprise, the management of which was God's major interest; they were God's people and their God was a living God, always thought of as intensely concerned with the actions and characters of people and nations. Each individual was a necessary item in a significant and divinely ordered cosmos. God has a personal interest in me, and has appointed work for me to do. If I am incapable of receiving his grace, it is unfortunate; but if that is God's will, who am I to complain? Yet while there's life, there's hope; and at any time

[1] William Ames (1576-1633) and William Perkins (1558-1602) were Puritan theologians who shared in the development of a "covenant" theology. For the connections between them and the founders of Massachusetts and a fuller description of the "covenant" theology, see Perry Miller, "The Marrow of Puritan Divinity," in *Errand into the Wilderness* (Cambridge, Mass., 1956).—Ed.

before death my risen Lord may whisper in my heart that I am of the blessed ones elected by his Father to salvation.

It is generally supposed that puritanism hampered intellectual and artistic activity; and there is some truth in this charge. Puritanism banned three forms in which the English excelled: the drama, religious music, and erotic poetry. Just why it banned the drama is still a matter of debate among the professors. Was it that the drama was supposed to lead to immorality, or because it amused people too much? Or simply because a number of the church fathers, like Chrysostom, had thundered against the pagan drama of their day? Whatever the reason, the puritan war on the theatre was hideously successful. There is no stranger phenomenon in literature than the swift rise of the English drama to a high zenith between 1580 and 1611, with Marlowe and Shakespeare; and its equally swift decline a few years after the death of Shakespeare. But it was not the puritans alone who killed the theatre. Their theological enemies, Bishop Laud and the high churchmen, were equally responsible. James I liked a good show as much as anyone and, as long as he reigned, the English theatre had court patronage; but Bishop Laud took charge of the conscience of Charles I, and discouraged the King from patronizing the drama as an object unworthy of a Christian monarch's support. Deprived both of middle-class and court patronage, the English theatre had no audience left but the sort that attends burlesque shows today; and the English theatre became not much better than burlesque shows. It was the puritans, to be sure, who closed the theatres; but one imagines that by 1642 the managers welcomed the closure, as it saved them from losing more money.

Although puritanism had nothing against music as such, the puritans injured music by taking it out of the churches. Religious exercises were stripped down to the bare rudiments of the days when early Christians met in secret, and would not have dared to play the organ, even if an organ had been available. Consequently instrumental music, like the other beautiful incidents with which the medieval church had enriched religious expression, was done away with for want of scriptural sanction, and because it was supposed to make the worshiper dreamy. To secular music (as Dr. Percy Scholes has shown in his recent work) the puritans had no objection; Oliver Cromwell kept an orchestra at his court, and the first Italian opera to be played in England was produced under his Protectorate, and by puritans.[2] A few musical instruments were brought to New England, and more were ordered in the latter part of the century. There was 'no law agin' it,' but music was not a form of activity that the English puritans cared much about, or were willing to make an effort to maintain in the New World.

I do not propose to hide the puritans behind the excuse that there was no room or opportunity for these things in a pioneer community. The German Moravians who came to Pennsylvania in the early eighteenth century maintained high musical standards because they believed that music was worth making some effort to keep up. And the puritans transplanted high educational standards for the same reason. Hard as colonial Americans worked, they, or some of them, had a certain leisure and surplus to devote to things of the spirit; and it depended entirely on their set of values what things of the spirit, if any, they chose to cultivate.

While the puritan wrote off certain cul-

[2] Percy A. Scholes, *The Puritans and Music in England and New England* (Oxford University Press, 1934).

tural activities such as the drama, and failed to do much for others, such as music, he was stimulated by his faith to an intellectual activity that was conspicuously absent in other English colonies. The alternative to a puritanically controlled intellectual life, in new settlements, was intellectual vacuity; the emphasis was on acquiring an estate. The 'best people' were engaged in growing tobacco or sugar cane, or trading with the natives; there was no incentive to lead a life of the spirit, no market for books, or audience for a play. At about the same time as the founding of New England, four other important English colonies—Virginia, Bermuda, Maryland, Barbados—and some lesser island plantations were established. Virginia by 1660 had a population almost equal to that of the whole of New England, and for wealth, Barbados was not far behind; neither was a puritan colony. But both colonies were singularly barren in literary production, although it may be that some hitherto hidden corpus of poetry, like that of Edward Taylor, or some prose manuscript of great merit, like Robert Beverley's *History of Virginia* (1705), may turn up. And where is the devotional poetry we might expect from Maryland, a Catholic colony? Why did not the scenic beauties of 'still-vext Bermoothes,' which at second hand lend such grace to Shakespeare's *Tempest*, inspire some native Bermudian to song, or prose?

Even in Mexico and Peru, where an enormously wealthy governing class existed almost a century before New England was founded, and whither learned ecclesiastics were constantly emigrating, nearly a century elapsed before a native intellectual life developed. The seventeenth century was the great age of Mexican and Peruvian literature; Don Pedro de Peralta Rocha Barnuevo y Benavídes, the savant of Lima, was almost contemporary with Cotton Mather—and Don Pedro was very much the same sort of indiscriminate and omniscient pedant as Don Cotton. But New England, within ten years of the founding of Massachusetts Bay, had a vigorous intellectual life of its own, expressed institutionally in a college, a school system, and a printing press; applied in a native sermon literature, poetry, and history. What is more, this life did not perish with the founders: it deepened and quickened as the century grew older, developing a scientific side. For in puritanism, New England had a great emotional stimulus to certain forms of intellectual life.

A humanist New England would doubtless have provided a pleasanter dwelling place, and a more sweet and wholesome stream to swell the American flood than a puritan New England. But there was no such alternative. Humanism is a tender plant, depending on a stable and leisured society, and on a nice adjustment of human relations, that cannot bear transplanting. As already noted, in a new country the natural alternative to intellectual puritanism is intellectual vacuity; and for a very good reason, that the mere physical labor of getting a living in a virgin country is so great as to exhaust and stultify the human spirit unless it have some great emotional drive. That, I take it, explains why in the nonpuritan colonies the humanist tradition of Elizabethan England shriveled; and why those colonies had to wait a century or more before they had any intellectual life worthy of the name. In South Carolina, we are told, the French planters of the end of the seventeenth century brought their Montaignes, and Montaigne is perhaps the best representative in old-world literature of a kindly, reflective, and disciplined humanism; yet the soil was unpropitious, and the tradition perished. Puritanism, on the contrary, throve under conditions of vigor, hardship, and isolation; hence the New England colonies were able almost immediately to create and support a distinct way of life that showed an unexpected vigor and virility long after English puritanism had been diluted or overwhelmed. The intellectual alternatives for New England, then, were not puritanism *or* humanism, but puritanism *or* overwhelming materialism, such as we find in typical newly settled regions whether English, French, Dutch, or Spanish.

Again we have a paradox. Puritanism in New England preserved far more of the humanist tradition that did non-puritanism in the other English colonies. The grammar schools and the college fostered a love of *literae humaniores*: Cicero, Virgil, Terence, and Ovid; Homer, Hesiod, and Theocritus. It was no small feat to keep alive the traditions of classical antiquity in a region that had never known the grandeur that was Rome, the glory that was Greece. The New England schools and colleges did just that; and handed down a priceless classical tradition, which has been mangled and trampled under foot by the professional educators and progressive pedagogues of the last hundred years. The classics flourished in New England under puritanism, and began to decay when puritanism withered.

The reason why the puritans nourished classicism while rejecting other aspects of Renaissance humanism was their concern for the education of posterity. Massachusetts Bay, New Haven, Connecticut, and Rhode Island were ruled both in church and state by men who had attended the British universities and the English grammar schools. A careful combing of lists of emigrants reveals that at least one hundred and thirty university alumni came to New England before 1646. This does not seem a very impressive total; but the entire population of New England in 1645 was not greater than 25,000, and probably less, which means that there was on the average one university-trained man to every forty or fifty families. In addition there was a large but indeterminate number of men who had a sound classical education in the English grammar schools, and therefore saw eye-to-eye with the university men on intellectual matters. These Oxford and Cambridge alumni, moreover, had an influence all out of proportion to their numbers. They were not concentrated in the seaports, but scattered all over the country, on the frontier and in country villages. Although they did not monopolize the political ruling class, since most of them were parsons, and as such ineligible to office, they did constitute an intellectual ruling class. Their standards were accepted by the community, and maintained in the college that they founded, largely for the purpose of perpetuating all that they understood by civilization. The intellectual life of New England was determined by the top layers of society; it was no proletarian cult welling up from the common people. *Accepted* by the community, not *imposed* on it, I say; for men of education were the chosen leaders of the puritan emigration. Deprived ministers or discontented country gentry gathered groups of neighbors, friends, and parishioners, emigrated in the same ship, and settled in the same place. They were the shepherds to whom the people looked for guidance and inspiration, on whose spoken words they hung, and whose written words they perused eagerly.

For the sources of New England intellectual life we must look to the English universities, and especially to the University of Cambridge. From the Middle Ages to the eighteenth century the main, almost the exclusive, scholarly preoccupation of the English universities was theology in both its aspects. The one was ecclesiastical polity, the form that the church should assume (including its relations to the state); the other was theology proper, or divinity—the philosophical aspect of Christianity, the relation of man and nature to God and the nature of God himself. There was next to no mathematical or scientific interest in the English universities until the Restoration; Barrow and Newton, who came after our time, were the first to give Cambridge her scientific reputation. Practically all the scientific discoveries of the seventeenth century were made outside the universities, which resisted each advance by a conservative adherence to Aristotelian physics and Ptolemaic astronomy. Medicine was not yet a university subject; young Englishmen studied it as apprentices to physicians or in Continental universities; nor was law. Englishmen read law at the Inns of Court. Universities did not foster creative literature; the great figures in Elizabethan literature were either men like Shakespeare who had merely a grammar-school education, or like Kit Marlowe and Milton, who regarded their college careers as a waste of time. Nor did the universities do much to foster creative scholarship outside the important branch of theology; the deep and fruitful labors of Renaissance humanists in collecting and editing texts of ancient classics went on outside university walls. The Bodleian Library was opened only in 1602, and a much longer time elapsed before Cambridge had a university library worthy of the name. Neither at Oxford nor at Cambridge in 1630 was there any teacher to compare with the Italian humanists of the *quattrocento*, or with the French school of classical scholars such as Scaliger, Casaubon, Lipsius, and Salmasius, or with Dutch university professors such as Heinsius and Grotius. The most that can be said is that university training in the liberal arts gave a solid background to men who already had the spark of creative genius in them—men such as Bacon, Spenser, Ben Jonson, and Donne.

The University of Cambridge as they knew it, not as it has since become, was the standard which the New England puritans attempted, however imperfectly, to attain. The names of her greatest masters, Ames and Perkins, Preston and Chaderton, were often on their lips, and always in their hearts. The beauty and serenity of the cloistered life there they looked back upon with an aching affection, when endeavoring in a frontier society of poverty and struggle to build up what they called their 'poor colledge in the wilderness.' And the intellectual life of Cambridge set the pace for the intellectual life of New England.

The English universities, in 1630 as in 1230, were regarded primarily as feeders to the church. Every holder of a college fellowship had to be in holy orders, the ambitious young men looked forward to becoming prelates; most of the students who took degrees intended to be clergymen. It is true that the English universities had, at the time of the Renaissance, opened their doors to young gentlemen of the leisured or the newly rich class, and provided for them a relatively easy course in ancient literature and history that led to no degree; and that this practice had so far become a tradition as to influence the New England college. But this class of young gentlemen, for the most part, had decidedly nonintellectual interests; they did not become tutors or professors or resident scholars; and their influence on the intellectual life of the university, like that of similar frivolous young men in our colleges today, was practically nil.

The one great, absorbing intellectual interest in the Oxford and Cambridge and Dublin from which the founders of New

England came was that very ecclesiastical controversy that drove them forth, in Lowell's words, 'to pitch new states as Old-World men pitch tents.' The contest between the Catholic and Protestant points of view, between men who wished to save what was left of the medieval church in the Anglican church, or restore what had been lost, and men who wished to strip off every medieval garment that could not be proved scriptural; the contest between the Arminian theology adumbrated by Archbishop Laud and Launcelot Andrewes and the quasi-Calvinist or 'Federal' theology expounded by Preston and Ames filled the British universities with contention and clamor. It is difficult to make a modern man appreciate the seventeenth-century interest in theology. Man's relation to God was a matter of great pith and moment to people in that era, and they needed no more compulsion to hear sermons that people now need compulsion to read newspapers. For one Englishman who had seen a play and for ten who had read one, there were literally hundreds who read theological literature, and thousands who listened intently to sermons. Theology was the leading topic of conversation around the campfires in Cromwell's army. Richard Baxter records that on a visit to the army in 1643 he found everyone talking about forms of prayer, infant baptism, free grace, free will, antinomianism, Arminianism, and liberty of conscience. The Reverend Mr. Baxter was so alarmed by the heterogeneity of religious opinion in the army that he gave up his quiet parish for an army chaplaincy in order to tell Cromwell's Ironsides what was what, and put the soldiers on the right track to salvation.

No subject of popular interest today, even economics, can compare in pervasiveness with the theology of the seventeenth century. Perhaps we can faintly grasp what theology meant to the people in those days if we imagine all parsons, priests, and rabbis turned out of our modern places of worship, and their places taken by economists who every Sabbath brought you the latest news from Washington, D. C., and told you just how you could escape taxes, or get a share of the divine (federal) bounty.

The puritans were the extreme wing of the Protestant party in the English universities, and the losing wing. They came to New England because they had lost every bout since 1570, when their great champion Cartwright was expelled from his chair of divinity at Cambridge. Until the reign of James I they thought that at least their theology was safe, since the Thirty-nine Articles of the Church of England were predominantly Calvinist; but James I discerned the antimonarchial implications of puritanism, high-church theologians began to interpret the Thirty-nine Articles in a reactionary manner, and through court influence puritans were expelled or excluded from posts of honor and emolument in the universities as in the government. This state of things, coming to a head in the years 1629-1634 with persecution, started the great puritan migration to New England. The educated men who organized and led this exodus brought with them a deep and lively interest in religion. The religious point of view dominated the intellectual life of New England for over a century, almost until the contest with England began.

A secondary intellectual interest in the Oxford and Cambridge of 1600 was poetry. All English schoolboys and college students were trained to write Latin and Greek verse; and at every marriage, birth, or death in the Royal Family, the choice wits of Oxford and Cambridge got out *epithalamia*, *gaudia*, or *threnodia* celebrating the happy or lamentable event in hexameters or elegiacs. It was an era of religious poetry, mostly by university-trained men—Spenser, Milton, Donne, Quarles, George Herbert, and, later, Cowley and Dryden. This tradition and, to a surprising extent, the amorous poetical fashion of Elizabeth's reign, crossed to New England together with other things of which the stricter puritans did not approve. For New England puritanism, like the Anglican Church of the Restoration, was a *via media*; a middle course between what Cotton Mather called the 'Rigid and High-flown Presbyterians' and the rigid sectaries and separatists. It never formally separated from the Church of England, as Roger Williams passionately believed it should. And New England puritanism had to make terms with humanity because it was in a responsible position. It has often been observed that political responsibility sobers down a fanatic, although of late examples to the contrary are numerous. When the emigrant puritans found themselves in a position of power in the New England colonies, they were neither so rigid nor so fanatical as one would suppose from the pamphlets they had written when out of power; and so in England itself when the Civil War brought the puritans on top.

It is not, then, correct to judge the puritans, as many writers have done, by the fanatical pamphlets of William Prynne, the Martin Marprelate tracts, and the writings of Richard Baxter. When in power they soon learned that no layman, however sincerely religious, could be expected to give all his waking moments to thoughts of God; that he must be given opportunity for earning a living, and for reasonable recreation, or, as they called it, 'seasonable merriment.' There was much opportunity for love and laughter in colonial New England, though not as much as there should have been. Thus, the puritans forbade the observance of Christmas, because of the pagan revelry that merry England had inflicted on the day of Christ's Nativity; but they established Thanksgiving Day which took its place; and now we have both Thanksgiving Day and Christmas. They abolished May Day, which in Elizabethan England was far from being the innocent schoolchildren's holiday that it is now; but instead they got two holidays in spring and early summer: election day and the college commencement, which soon took on the character of a Flemish kermis. They attempted to regulate the liquor traffic; but they never attempted or even suggested a complete prohibition of all alcoholic beverages. Indeed, it might be agreed that puritan restrictions on purely physical enjoyment tended to stimulate intellectual life; that a good many people who in England would have lingered in a tavern, carousing and singing songs, stayed at home and wrote prose and poetry, or argued over the fine points of the last sermon and picked flaws in their parson's theology!

One must also keep in mind the small and thinly populated area of which we are speaking. The estimates of the United States Census Bureau give the New England colonies 17,800 people in 1640; 106,000 at the end of the century. As a basis of comparison, Virginia and Maryland combined had about the same population as New England from 1660 to the close of the century. Boston, the largest town in the English colonies, had about 7,000 people by 1690. It would be absurd to expect so thinly populated and isolated a province to produce poets of the caliber of Milton and Dryden, or prose writers equal to Lord Clarendon and John Locke. We must remember what is to be reasonably expected of a community of 25,000 to 100,000 people, agricultural for the most part, having no leisure class, or ready means of wealth, or method of conserving inherited property. New England was a poor country, even by the standards of the day, struggling with a niggardly nature for livelihood, subject to the constant tendency of the frontier to reduce humanity to a dead level of ambition and intellect. Under such circumstances we should not expect anything very great, original, or creative; for no new colony, since those of ancient Greece, has been able, during the period of adjustment to a new environment, to equal the intellectual achievement of its mother country. I am inviting you to accompany me in a survey of a small group of people striving manfully, even heroically, to achieve an ideal—an ideal not merely religious, though permeated by religion; an ideal of transmitting a civilization, and of planting in the New World the very vines whose fruit they had enjoyed in the Old. As New Englanders themselves were wont to say, 'Despise not the day of small things.'

Perhaps it is his English background that enables ALAN SIMPSON (1912-) to write about the Puritans from a point of view that does not place him in any school of interpretation. Now president of Vassar College and a historian, Simpson builds upon the revisionists even while correcting their emphasis upon the intellectuality of Puritanism. For him, the conversion experience is not only the real mark of the Puritan; it is also the key to understanding the dynamics of the Puritan movement. Why did Puritanism splinter into a left and a right? To which side did the founders of Massachusetts belong?*

The Conversion Experience and Church Reform

How does one define Puritanism? No doubt there is a sense in which Puritanism can be found in the Middle Ages or in civilizations other than our own; but I am concerned here with the historic experiences from which the name derives. It began as a sneer, was taken up in self-defense, and has established itself as a convenient label. But historians have differed widely in its usage. There is one tradition which restricts it to the more orthodox branches represented by Presbyterianism in England and Congregationalism in New England. Boston, with a vested interest in its own respectability, has often inclined to this usage. There is another tradition which extends it through the Center and Left of the movement but stops short at the Quakers. For my own part, if I am looking at the movement as a whole, I can see little reason for excluding the Quakers. An enterprise which began in the sixteenth century by exhorting men to prepare themselves for a miracle of grace and ended by asserting the presence of the Holy Spirit in every individual is one movement. If it has many stopping places en route, it has a logical terminus. If one movement requires one label, and if one is not to go to the trouble of inventing a new one, I am content to apply the term "Puritan" to the whole of it. However, it is not

*Reprinted from *Puritanism in Old and New England* by Alan Simpson by permission of the University of Chicago Press. Copyright 1955 by the University of Chicago. The University of Chicago, 1955. Footnotes omitted.

the name that matters but the unity, or continuity of experience, that underlies the labels.

What was it that they all shared? The formal answer is dissatisfaction within the established church—the church established by Queen Elizabeth as the English answer to the problems created by the Reformation, the middle way between Rome and Geneva. This answer is true enough but not the most revealing. A better answer is one which seizes on the religious experience from which the dissatisfaction springs. The essence of Puritanism—what Cromwell called the "root of the matter" when he surveyed the whole unruly flock—is an experience of conversion which separates the Puritan from the mass of mankind and endows him with the privileges and the duties of the elect. The root of the matter is always a new birth, which brings with it a conviction of salvation and a dedication to warfare against sin.

There is no difficulty in discovering what this experience involved. The whole object of the Puritan's existence was to trace its course in himself and to produce it in others. He develops it in his sermons, systematizes it in his creeds, charts it in his diaries. Of innumerable examples, let me describe the experience of Thomas Goodwin; rather, let me summarize his own description. He wrote it, of course, for edification; and, if it was not published in his lifetime, we can easily imagine how many sermons were based on it and how many students of Magdalen College, over which he eventually presided, were given the opportunity of benefiting from it.

The Goodwin home, in which he was brought up, had its face set in the right direction. The family stance seems to have been like that of Bunyan's Pilgrim, with the burden on his back, the Book in his hands, and the cry ringing in his ears, "What shall I do to be saved?" At six, young Thomas was warned by a servant that, if he did not repent of his sins, Hell awaited him. At seven, he had learned to weep for them and look for the signs of grace. At twelve, he thought he had more grace than anyone else in his village. At thirteen, he went up to Christ's College, Cambridge, and attached himself, as an eager learner, to the more mature laborers in the vineyard. He learned of the ministries of Perkins and Ames. He heard of famous conversions. He joined the spiritual exercises which the faculty held in their rooms. He was taught, with other students, how to test the state of his soul. This was the life which he was to try to institutionalize in Oxford under the Cromwellian government and which a profane generation was to describe as Goodwin's scruple-shop; but meanwhile he was a beginner and for many years a beginner oscillating between hope and despair. For the real experience had not yet come.

He kept on thinking he had it, only to find himself deceived. He could go through all the cycle of self-examination, repentance, exaltation, and good works, only to discover that the sense of assurance evaporated. The elect kept their assurance. The doctrine not only said so: one had only to look at them to see. But he lost his. For a time Arminianism offered its consolations. Arminianism was that doctrine of free will which was asserting itself everywhere as a reaction against predestination and was coming to be the distinguishing mark of the official piety at the time Goodwin was a student. For a time this Arminianism seemed to square with his experience. If the human will was not enslaved by sin but free to choose, he ought to expect the sense of assurance to fluctuate. But in his heart he knew that Arminianism was wrong because the holy youths do not fall away. They persevere, showing that God has indeed seized them. At this point he faltered in his pilgrimage and surrendered, as he tells us, to his characteristic sin. If salvation eluded him, success was well within his reach. The holy preachers like Dr. Sibbes, the holy converts like Mr. Price, the holy tutors, and the holy students could go on brooding over their consciences. Thomas Goodwin would stick to a fashionable style and make his mark.

He explains that he was saved from the consequences of this depraved decision by the real experience. It came to him, of course, through the medium of a sermon: the normal means employed by God to hammer the hardened heart. The text was "Defer not thy repentance." As he describes it, the characteristic features of the experience emerge. He is completely passive, for this is a Divine power exerted on a soul which is incapable of helping itself. He is shown *how* incapable by a revelation of his unworthiness which distinguishes the real thing from previous illusions. He compares the light shed by grace upon the state of a natural man's soul with the light of the sun piercing into the depths of a filthy dungeon to reveal a floor crawling with vermin. Always before, when he wept for his sins, he had kept some feeling of human merit. Now he knows he has none; that the natural man, even when seemingly a good man, is only a beautiful abomination, for the natural man has had no merit since Adam's disobedience, and Hell is his just destination. Then, in the midst of this horror, comes the act of mercy: the voice that says to the dead soul, "Arise and live." Goodwin compares himself to a traitor whom a king has pardoned and then raised to the position of friend and favorite. But, if the favorite has tremendous privileges, he also has tremendous duties. His life must be an endless war against the sin which dishonors his sovereign and an endless effort to be the means of producing in others that experience which has freed himself.

I could, of course, have chosen better-known personages than Thomas Goodwin, for there is almost no famous Puritan who has not left some account of this experience, even though it is only, as in Cromwell's case, a few haunted lines written to a cousin in the midst of his travail. I chose Goodwin because he is typical, because he is writing deliberately for imitation, and because he illustrates one of the characteristic weaknesses of the Puritan character—its want of proportion.

However Puritans differ, they all have something in common with Thomas Goodwin. They separate the world of nature from the world of grace. They insist that the natural man cannot grow in grace; he has to be reborn. They explain the rebirth as a vivid personal experience in which the individual soul encounters the wrath and redemptive love of God. It is an experience for which the church may prepare a man, and after which it may claim to guide him, but which in its essential nature is beyond the church's control. They describe the new creature in the language appropriate to a special destiny: he is the elect, the chosen, the favorite, the peculiar people, the saint. They extol the liberty of the new creature, by which they mean the gift of eternal life, and the freedom which the regenerate may claim on earth under Divine law. It is the duty of the saint to search out that law and live by it, and, no matter how much they differ, they are agreed about one thing. It demands discipline. The discipline of self-trial—the perpetual self-accusation of the Puritan diaries; the discipline of self-denial—the massive prohibitions of the Puritan code; the discipline which Milton found in Cromwell when he said he could conquer the world because he had first conquered himself. In later generations what they were talking about could be confused with respectability; but in these days it was a holy violence under compression. Finally, they derive this view of life from the Scriptures, which they regard as the sole source of authority—the complete rule by which men must live—though we shall see later how some regenerate spirits contrive to escape from this initial limitation.

This doctrine of salvation was a logical development, on English soil, of the Protestant doctrines of predestination, justification by faith, and the all-sufficiency of the Scriptures. Whether it stems, as older historians were content to say, from Calvinism or, as we now tend to say, from Rhineland Protestantism, it is enough to recognize that, in the opinion of those who held it, the whole movement of history which we call the Reformation, and which they regarded as a Divine liberation of the church from centuries of superstition, was intended to have this result.

They lived, however, in a society which obviously thought otherwise. When the Puritan looked around him in Elizabethan England, he saw two kinds of wickedness: the wickedness of people who were living without any benefit from religion and the wickedness of people who had embraced the wrong religion. The first class had always been a considerable section of mankind in the most Christian centuries. In this century of religious confusion, social disturbance, intellectual speculation, and fierce acquisitive energy, godlessness confronted the Puritan in every walk of life. He met it on the Elizabethan roads, in those rogues and vagabonds who exemplified the modern problem of poverty. He met it in the underworld of the overgrown capital. He heard it in the announcement of businessmen that clergymen ought not to meddle with a merchant's business. Ordinary humanity in its alehouse; the crowd that thronged the Shakespearean theater; the intellects released from Christian tradition; the court with its worship of beauty, wit, honor, power, and fame—all seemed dedicated to the proposition that men are created without a soul to be saved or damned. Some insight into this world—or at least into its less sophisticated reaches—is provided by a list of thirty-two popular errors which William Perkins, a founder of the Puritan discipline, catalogued for the instruction of the ignorant. It is a comprehensive indictment of the profane, the cheerful, the superstitious, the free-enterprisers, and the people who thought it enough to be good citizens. Here are some of the items in this syllabus of errors:

"Drinking in the alehouse is good fellowship and shews a good kind nature, and maintains neighbourhood."

"Howsoever a man live, yet if he call upon God on his death bed, and say Lord have mercy upon me, and so go away like a lamb, he is certainly saved."

"Merry ballads and books, such as *Scogin, Bevis of Southampton*, etc., are good to drive away time and remove heart qualms."

"A man may go to wizards, called wisemen, for counsel; because God hath provided a salve for every sore."

"Every man must be for himself and God for us all."

"A man may make of his own [property] whatsoever he can."

"If a man be no adulterer, no thief, nor murderer, and do no man harm, he is a right honest man."

This last seems an innocent sentiment until we recall that from Perkins' point of view this man is simply a beautiful abomination so long as he remains an unconverted soul.

This unregenerate world would not be

allowed to flaunt its wickedness if religion were rightly understood. But what was the official religion? The Puritan found himself confronted by that Anglican piety which had developed side by side, and in conflict with his own, within the framework of the Establishment erected by Queen Elizabeth. The famous settlement of the first year of her reign had left a great deal unsettled, but the complexion which it finally acquired was thoroughly frustrating to the Puritan. He believed in the total depravity of nature; he was told that men were not so fallen as he thought they were. He believed that the natural man had to be virtually reborn; he was told that he could grow in grace. He believed that the sermon was the only means of bringing saving knowledge and that the preacher should speak as a dying man to dying men. He was told that there were many means of salvation, that sermons by dying men to dying men were often prolix, irrational, and socially disturbing, and that what they had to say that was worth saying had usually been better said in some set form that could be read aloud. He demanded freedom for the saints to exercise their gifts of prayer and prophecy, only to be told that the needs of the community were better met by the forms of common prayer. He felt instinctively that the church was where Christ dwelt in the hearts of the regenerate. He was warned that such feelings threatened the prudent distinction between the invisible church of the saved and the visible church of the realm. He insisted that the church of the realm should be judged by Scripture, confident that Scripture upheld him, and prepared to assert that nothing which was not expressly commanded in Scripture ought to be tolerated in the church. He was told that God had left much to the discretion of human reason; that this reason was exercised by public authority, which in England was the same for both church and state; and that whatever authority enjoined, in its large area of discretion, ought to be loyally obeyed.

Obviously what we have here is a reconstruction of a Catholic tradition within the framework of a national Protestant church. As stated here, it is derived from Richard Hooker, who was writing at a time when most Anglican bishops still subscribed to that theology of predestination whose implications the Puritans were rigorously pursuing. But the Establishment had clearly refused to take this path, and before long they adopted the Arminianism which was much more congenial to them.

The effect of these tendencies on the Puritan can easily be imagined. Such a church had misconceived the "root of the matter." At best, it was a halfway house between a corrupt and a pure church; at worst, it was barely distinguishable from Rome. It was not run by saints; it was not organized for the production of saints; and it did not repress the world's wickedness.

What were the elect to do? The first thing they could do was to organize, using every available means for the infiltration of English life and the conversion of authority to their point of view. They had plenty of opportunities, both in the early days, when the character of the settlement was relatively undetermined, and later. The powers which could be brought to bear on dissidents in this society were limited even when fully deployed. Aristocracy imposed its shelter between the individual and the state; so did corporate bodies like the universities, the Inns of Court, the commercial companies, and the municipalities. Above all, Parliament was open to the efforts of the Reformers, and, though the sovereign's disfavor for any interference with his ecclesiastical supremacy was obvious enough, there were hopes that he might see the light. Could he resist the plain word of God? So for three generations Puritans organized, with a base in the universities, a grip on the press, a connection in the country houses and the counting-houses, and a party in Parliament. It was an advancing frontier of preachers, converts, and patrons, checked by many features in the social topography but always pushing forward to its goal—the completion of a half-finished Reformation.

Naturally, one asks what made people receptive to such a demanding view of life, and naturally there have been suggestions that this doctrine of salvation was somehow connected with the aspirations of social classes. We have been told, with varying degrees of crudity and subtlety, that Puritanism was the ideology of the bourgeoisie. On that subject there are two simple observations to be made. First, Puritanism never offered itself as anything but a doctrine of salvation, and it addressed itself neither directly nor indirectly to social classes but to man as man. Second, its attractions as a commitment were such that it made converts in all classes—among aristocrats, country gentry, businessmen, intellectuals, freeholders, and small tradesmen. Earls were linked with tinkers in the fraternity of converted souls. However, some of the preachers' seed fell on stony ground, and some fell on ground in which it would never have germinated without artificial stimulants. High society and slum society were, on the whole, stony ground. So also were the field laborers, for the reasons that Baxter, who knew his parish as well as any clergyman in England, pointed out. Puritanism was the religion of a Book, and, without opportunity to master the Book and to engage in mutual criticism and edification around it, it was hard to make any progress. Weavers at their looms, tradesmen in their shops, and yeomen farmers in their homes could be organized, but not so easily the peasant in the field.

The fertilized ground was the ground which for one reason or another was out of sympathy with official policy: noblemen out of favor at court and ready to play with Puritanism as a weapon or a consolation; country gentry having a hard time making ends meet during a century of inflation; city men irritated by royal or episcopal regimentation or casting their eyes on church lands; self-made men in rural industry who smarted under the snubs of neighboring gentry; rural craftsmen for whom there was either no church at all or some country tippler mumbling a prayer between visits to the alehouse; and Englishmen in all classes when the strongest national prejudice—fear of popery—swept across them and it looked as though safety lay in embracing the other extreme. Genuine Puritans, as I have defined them, were never more than a small minority, but there was plenty of discontent on which they could feed, and the movement grew with the years as the country headed toward a crisis in the relations between king and Parliament. The growth of a constitutional opposition to the Stuart monarchy had a separate origin from the Puritan movement, but it naturally furnished the Puritan with his best hope of procuring a reform of the church.

However, the more persistently the Puritan organized, the clearer it became that his attempt to remodel the church would be resisted to the limit of the government's capacity. Elizabeth had administered the first checks when the tendencies of the movement became plain. Once Puritans began to argue that church and state must be separated in England to the extent of putting the church on its scriptural basis, they ran into unflinching resistance. This was to separate the inseparable; to make the head of the state a member of some sort of Presbyterian church; and to place the state, in the final analysis, at the mercy of the interpreters of the Divine Will. However much they might protest that the monarchy had nothing to fear and everything to gain from a partnership with a scriptural church, Elizabeth knew better and suppressed them. Her successor, James I, who had had his own experience of Presbyterianism, followed suit with that mixture of hard words and half-hearted action that served him as a policy. Charles I put Archbishop Laud in charge. By 1630, when a wit was asked by a puzzled inquirer what the Arminians held—Arminianism being the badge of the Laudian party—he was able to reply, "All the best bishoprics and deaneries in England." By that time, too, the partnership of king and bishop was "going it alone." Parliamentary government had been suspended after three unworkable Parliaments, and all the means of coercion were being marshaled against the Puritan allies of the constitutional opposition.

The reaction of the Puritans to this prolonged experience of frustration varied with the individual. It was their duty to search for the Will of God, which meant scanning his commands in Scripture, or applying to Scripture such reason as grace had restored, or following the lead of the spirit which dwelt in their hearts. What was the duty of a regenerate soul under an unregenerate government which persisted in maintaining a corrupt church? One reaction came early. It was nothing less than the fragmentation of the movement—the earliest symptoms of that process of fission which was to run through the whole history of Puritanism. The first impulse of the movement had been to think in terms of a national church, directed by the elite but embracing all members of the community: some English counterpart to the reformed churches of Scotland or the Continent. This continued to be the hope of the majority and eventually expressed itself in English Presbyterianism: the Puritanism of the Right. But in others frustration precipitated a potentiality inherent in the idea of election: the tendency to segregate the elite from the mass and to substitute for the traditional idea of a church coextensive with society the idea of a church as a covenanted body of saints. This was that pressure to identify the visible and the invisible church which figures so prominently in the Center and Left of the Puritan movement.

The impulse might be carried some way or all the way. Carried to its fullest extent, it meant separation: the duty to separate from the polluted mass of mankind. So little groups of saints peel off from the national church under the leadership of a minister to meet surreptitiously in each other's houses, to migrate to the Netherlands if England is made too uncomfortable for them, and to experience, wherever they go, the perplexities as well as the privileges of their strange adventure. Along this route, hovering between separation and some sense of communion with the church they had left, went the Pilgrim Fathers. Others were less fortunate in their leadership. After beginning by reducing the church to a voluntary association, they ended by reducing it to a collection of individuals, each of whom had separated from the other's corruptions. And so the Reformation achieved one of its logical possibilities, with the individual becoming a church in himself.

The same impulse carried only part way rejected separation and continued to think in terms of an orthodoxy imposed on the community; but the ecclesiastical medium would be an association of covenanted churches, each composed of individuals who could give satisfactory evidence of their conversion. A succession of distinguished figures in this tradition also migrated to the Netherlands, to work out there, so far as English and Dutch authority permitted, some of the implications of what we have come to call Nonseparating Congregationalism.

In this way, lines of fragmentation were being etched out in the years of opposition. On the Right, the future Presbyterians; in the Center, the future Congregationalists; on the Left, the Separating Congregationalists. In England, where all plans for the future of church government had to be subordinated to the struggle for survival of a preaching ministry, the distinctions might be blurred. Abroad, where the tasks of organization had to be faced, they emerged more sharply.

A conception of Puritanism as a repressive code of life appeared in both popular and scholarly books written during the 1920s. Among the scholars hostile to Puritanism, none is more influential than JAMES TRUSLOW ADAMS (1878-1949), whose history of seventeenth-century New England, *The Founding of New England*, won a Pulitzer Prize in 1922. Adams approached Puritanism in the manner of a muckraker; he would expose the truth that the filiopietists had covered up. Like many other historians of the 1920s, Adams believed that economic aspects were a determining factor in the course of history. How does Adams employ the concept of class conflict to explain the development of government in early Massachusetts?*

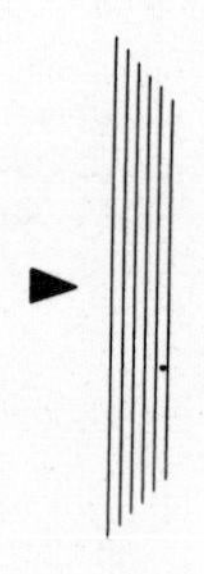

Economic Interests and Political Conflict

During the years that the Pilgrims had thus been struggling to found a tiny commonwealth on an inhospitable bit of the long American coast-line, events had been moving rapidly on the more crowded stage of the Old World. In France, the power of the Huguenots had been hopelessly crushed by the fall of Rochelle in 1628; while in England, affairs were evidently approaching a crisis, due to the incompetence of the government of Charles, with its disgraceful military failures abroad, and its illegal financial exactions at home. No one was safe from the ruin of his fortune or the loss of his freedom. The nobility and gentry, subject to the imposition of forced loans, faced imprisonment if they refused to pay; and those below the rank of gentleman were the unwilling hosts of a horde of ruffians, the unpaid and frequently criminal soldiery returned from unsuccessful foreign ventures, and billeted upon them by the government. The laws against Catholics were largely suspended to please the Queen, who was of that faith, and the prospects were daily growing darker for the Puritan and patriot elements, both within and without the Church. Religious toleration as an avowed governmental policy was not, as yet, seriously considered by any considerable body of men outside of Holland, the notable example of which

*From James Truslow Adams, *The Founding of New England* (Boston: Little Brown & Company, 1921), pp. 118-124, 134-145. Reprinted with omission of some footnotes by permission of Mrs. James Truslow Adams.

country had failed to influence England, where the control of the church was evidently passing into the hands of Laud and his party. The time had thus come when the King must face a united opposition of the soundest men in the country—of those who feared alike for their property, their liberty, and their religion.

The formation of the Puritan party, drawing into its fold men animated by any or all of these motives, in varying proportions, coincided with the beginning of the great increase in emigration to Massachusetts, which was to carry twenty thousand persons to the shores of New England between 1630 and 1640. But if attention is concentrated too exclusively upon the history of the continental colonies in North America, and, more particularly, of those in New England, the impression is apt to be gained that this swarming out of the English to plant in new lands was largely confined to Massachusetts and its neighbors, and to the decade named. The conclusion, drawn from these false premises has naturally been that Puritanism, in the New England sense, was the only successful colonizing force. We do not wish to minimize the value of any deeply felt religious emotion in firmly planting a group of people in a new home. . . .The Puritan colonies, nevertheless, not only were far from being the only permanent ones, but themselves were not always equally successful; and it is well to point out that many elements, besides peculiarity of religious belief, entered into the success of the New England colonies, as contrasted with the conspicuous failure of the Puritan efforts in the Carribbean.

At the beginning of the increased emigration to Massachusetts, colonizing, indeed, had ceased to be a new and untried business. To say nothing of the numerous large and small French, Dutch, and Spanish settlements firmly established in the New World, and the English already planted on the mainland, the latter nation had successfully colonized the islands of Bermuda in 1612, St. Kitts in 1623, Barbadoes and St. Croix in 1625, and Nevis and Barbuda three years later. By the time John Winthrop led his band to the shores of Massachusetts Bay, besides the five hundred Dutch in New Amsterdam, ten thousand Englishmen were present, for six months of each year, in Newfoundland, engaged in the fisheries there; nine hundred had settled permanently in Maine and New Hampshire; three hundred within the present limits of Massachusetts; three thousand in Virginia; between two and three thousand in Bermuda; and sixteen hundred in Barbadoes; while the numbers in the other colonies are unknown. The figures are striking also for the year 1640, or slightly later, at which date the tide is too often considered as having flowed almost wholly toward the Puritan colonies of New England for the preceding ten years. The number in Massachusetts at that time had risen to fourteen thousand, in Connecticut to two thousand, and in Rhode Island to three hundred. Maine and New Hampshire however, contained about fifteen hundred, Maryland the same number, Virginia nearly eight thousand, Nevis about four thousand, St. Kitts twelve to thirteen thousand, and Barbadoes eighteen thousand six hundred. There are no contemporary figures for Barbuda, St. Croix, Antigua, Montserrat, and other settlements. At the end, therefore, of what has often been considered a period of distinctly Puritan emigration, we find that approximately only sixteen thousand Englishmen had taken their way to the Puritan colonies, as against forty-six thousand to the others; which later figure, moreover, is undoubtedly too low, owing to the lack of statistics just noted. Nor does the above statement take into account the thousands of Englishmen who emigrated to Ireland during the same period, and whose motives were probably similar to those animating the emigrants to the New World, however different their destinations may have been. There had, indeed, been a "great migration," resulting in an English population in America and the West Indies, by 1640 or thereabout, of over sixty-five thousand persons; but it is somewhat misleading to apply the term solely to the stream of emigrants bound for the Puritan colonies, who were outnumbered three to one by those who went to settlements where religion did not partake of the "New England way." Although young John Winthrop might write of his brother that it "would be the ruine of his soule to live among such company" as formed the colony of Barbadoes in 1629, nevertheless, the population of that island had risen to nearly nineteen thousand in another decade, whereas that of Massachusetts had reached only fourteen thousand.

If, in addition, we recall the fact that, approximately, not more than one in five of the adult males who went even to Massachusetts was sufficiently in sympathy with the religious ideas there prevalent to become a church member, though disfranchised for not doing so, we find that in the "great migration" the Puritan element, in the sense of New England church-membership, amounted to only about four thousand persons out of about sixty-five thousand. In the wider sense, indeed, Puritanism, in its effect on legal codes and social usages, is found present, in greater or less degree, in almost all the colonies, island and mainland, but the influence of the form that it took in New England was to be wholly disproportionate upon the nation which evolved from the scattered continental settlements.

If, however, we shift from our usual point of view and, instead of studying the English emigration of the time in the light of the leaders who reached New England, consider the great body of those who left the shores of England, we shall have to account for those fourteen emigrants out of every fifteen, who, although willing to leave their homes and all they had held dear, yet shunned active participation in the Bible Commonwealths. It is evident that other causes, besides the quarrels in the Church and the tyranny of Laud, must have been operative on a large scale, to explain the full extent of the movement. It seems probable that the principal cause that induced such an extraordinary number of people, from the ranks of the lesser gentry and those below them, to make so complete a break in their lives as was implied by leaving all they had ever known for the uncertainties of far-off lands, was economic. They came for the simple reason that they wanted to better their condition. They wanted to be rid of the growing and incalculable exactions of government. They wanted to own land; and it was this last motive, perhaps, which mainly had attracted those twelve thousand persons out of sixteen thousand who swelled the population of Massachusetts in 1640, but were not church members; for the Puritan colonies were the only ones in which land could be owned in fee simple, without quit-rent or lord, and in which it was freely given to settlers.

The local sources in England of the great migration, and the relations of that movement to local economc conditions, have not received adequate treatment as yet, and the subject is somewhat obscure; but apparently it was the eastern and southeastern counties that furnished the main supply of immigrants for the New World. It was in these counties that the artisans from Flanders had sought refuge, when driven abroad by Alva, as well as the Huguenots from France. In these counties, also, the enclosures, which were of such far-reaching economic influence, had taken place earlier than elsewhere, while wages there showed a lower ratio to subsistence than in the north. The special area in which the inhabitants were most disposed to seek new homes was that around the low country draining into the Wash; and throughout the early seventeenth century economic and agrarian agitation was notably constant in that particular region, the period of heaviest emigration—that between 1630 and 1640—marking, perhaps, its years of greatest economic readjustment and strain. The rise in rents and land-values had, indeed, been enormous during the preceding half-century. But this agricultural prosperity had been so closely bound up with the great expansion of the cloth industry, that in this section it may be said to have been wholly dependent upon it. From 1625 to 1630, however, the business of the clothiers suffered a very severe decline, which continued for some years, and the effects of which were very marked in the agricultural industries as well. In Norwich, for example, the Mayor and Aldermen complained that, owing to the dearth of food, and to the great increase of unemployment due to bad trade conditions, the amount necessary for poor relief had to be doubled. Moreover, as is always the case in periods of great economic alteration, the change had not affected all classes in the community alike. The yeomanry, who were less influenced by the rapidly rising scale of living, and so could save a much larger proportion of their increased gains from the high agricultural prices, were improving their position at the expense of the gentry. Enterprising traders, in the cloth and other industries, who had acquired fortunes, but who naturally were not of the old families, were pushing in and buying country estates, and, like all *nouveaux riches*, were asserting their new and unaccustomed position by raising the scale of living. Many of the gentry, on the other hand, unable to adjust themselves to the new economic conditions or to take advantage of them, and yet unwilling to give up their comparative position in the county, found themselves "overtaken," as a contemporary writer says, "with too well meaning and good nature," and so were "inforced sometimes to suffer a revolution" in their domestic affairs. About the years of the emigration, however, there seem to have been financial difficulties and economic unrest among all the classes, due to the immediate crisis in the cloth trade, as well as the more general conditions of the time. . . .

John Winthrop, now [1629] in his forty-third year, who was living the life of a country squire at Groton, in Suffolk, and was a small office-holder under government, had been anxiously watching the course of affairs. Of a sensitive and deeply religious nature, strongly attached to the Puritan cause, he could not but regard the future with the greatest anxiety. "The Lord hath admonished, threatened, corrected and astonished us," he wrote to his wife in May, 1629, "yet we growe worse and worse, so as his spirit will not allwayes strive with us, he must needs give waye to his fury at last. . . . We sawe this, and humbled not ourselves, to turne from our evill wayes, but have provoked him more than all the nations rounde about us: therefore he is turninge the cuppe toward us also, and because we are the last, our portion must be, to drinke the verye dreggs which remaine. My dear wife, I am veryly persuaded, God will bringe some heavye Affliction upon this lande, and that speedylye." In addition to his fear that all hope of civil, as well as of even a moderate degree of religious, liberty was rapidly fading, Winthrop was also much troubled by the prospects for his personal social and financial position. A few months earlier, he had written to his son Henry, at that time a settler in Barbadoes, that he then owed more than he was able to pay without selling his land; and throughout all his letters and papers of the period runs the same strain of anxiety over money matters. Although possessed of a modest estate, which when subsequently sold, realized £4200, the demands of a large family, and the increased cost of living, were more than he could meet. In June, he was, in addition, deprived of his office under the Master of the Wards, and wrote to his wife that "where we shall spende the rest of or short tyme I knowe not: the Lorde, I trust, will direct us in mercye."

. . .It was natural that Winthrop should seriously consider the thought of emigrating. Just at this time, a paper consisting of arguments for and against settling a plantation in New England was being circulated. . . . The reasons given in favor of it were mainly religious and economic. The first dwelt upon the glory of opposing Anti-Christ, in the form of the French Jesuits in Canada, and of raising "a particular church" in New England, while the second referred to the supposed surplus population at home, and to the standard and cost of living which had "growne to that height of intemperance in all excesse of Riott, as noe mans estate allmost will suffice to keepe saile with his aequalls."

The document, which has come down to us in at least four different forms, was possibly drafted by Winthrop himself, though the evidence is only inferential, and it has also been attributed to the Reverend John White and others. It is interesting to note that John Hampden wrote to Sir John Eliot, then in prison, for a copy of it. Whether or not Winthrop was the author, several copies, one of them indorsed "May, 1629," contain memoranda of "Particular considerations in the case of J. W.," in which he wrote that the success of the plan had come to depend upon him, for "the chiefe supporters (uppon whom the rest depends) will not stirr without him," and that his wife and children are in favor of it. "His meanes," moreover, he wrote, "heer are so shortened (now 3 of his sonnes being com to age have drawen awaie the one half of his estate) as he shall not be able to continue in that place and imployment where he now iss, his ordinary charg being still as great almost as when his meanes was double"; and that "if he lett pass this opportunitie, That talent wch God hath bestowed uppon him for publicke service is like to be buried." "With what comfort can I live," he added in one version, "wth 7 or 8 servts in that place and condition where for many years I have spent 3: or 400 li yearly and maintained a greater chardge?" The prospects in England, for his wife and children, lay heavily on his mind. "For my care of thee and thine," he wrote to the former, after the die was cast, "I will say nothing. The Lord knows my heart, that it was one great motive to draw me into this course.". . .

Winthrop's reasons have been thus dwelt upon, because, in the motives given by him who was the purest, gentlest, and broadest-minded of all who were to guide the destinies of the Bay Colony, we presumably find the highest of those which animated any of the men who sought its shores. As we descend the scale of character, the religious incentives narrow and disappear, as does also the desire for honorable public service, and the economic factor alone remains.

In July, a few weeks after Winthrop lost his office, Isaac Johnson, a brother-in-law of the Earl of Lincoln, wrote to Emanuel Downing, a brother-in-law of Winthrop, asking them to meet at Sempringham, the

Earl's seat in Lincolnshire, whither they both went on the 28th. There they undoubltedly met Dudley, Johnson, Humphrey, and others of that family and social group.[1] All those gathered there, so far as we know, were keenly interested in the project for Massachusetts. As they were also in close touch with Warwick, Rich, and others of those who were just at the moment planning to send out the colony to Providence in September, it is probable that both places were considered, and Warwick continued for years to urge Winthrop and his group to move to the southern colony. The decision, however, was in favor of Massachusetts; and, a few weeks later, on August 26, Saltonstall, Dudley, Johnson, Humphrey, Winthrop, and seven others, signed an agreement by which they bound themselves to be ready, with their families and goods, by the first of the following March, to embark for New England, and to settle there permanently.

There was one clause in the agreement, of incalculable importance. "Provided always," so it read, "that before the last of September next, the whole Government, together with the patent for the said plantation, be first, by an order of court, legally transferred and established to remain with us and others which shall inhabit upon the said Plantation." Possibly as a result of consultation with the Cambridge signers, Governor Cradock, at a meeting of the court of the Company a month earlier, had read certain propositions, "conceived by himself," which anticipated this condition. They seem to have struck those present as serious and novel, and of such importance in their possible consequences as to call for deferred consideration in great secrecy. The matter was brought up at a number of successive meetings, and it was only after much debate, objections on the part of many, and the taking of legal advice, that the court finally voted that the charter and government might be removed to America. By such transfer, and the use made of the charter in New England, what was intended to be a mere trading company, similar to those which had preceded it, became transformed into a self-governing commonwealth, whose rulers treated the charter as if it were the constitution of an independent state. Such an interpretation could not legally be carried beyond a certain point, and the attempt was bound to break down under the strain.

The step, in its far-reaching consequences, was one of the most important events in the development of the British colonies, but its story remains a mystery. It was a completely new departure, but may have been suggested to the leaders by the act of the Pilgrims in buying out their English partners and thus in effect, though without any legal authority, constituting themselves a self-governing community. There has been much discussion as to whether the absence in the original charter of any words indicating that the corporation was to remain in England was due to accident or design. It is impossible to prove the point either way, for Winthrop's statement, of somewhat uncertain application and written many years later, does not seem conclusive against the other facts and probabilities. The proceedings at the meetings of the court show clearly, at least, that many of the most active patentees had had no inkling of any such conscious alteration of the document at the time of issue, nor does it seem likely that Charles I would have knowingly consented. If the charter were intentionally so worded as to

[1] The family and social group centered around the Earl of Lincoln played an important role in organizing the Massachusetts-Bay Company. Thomas Dudley was the Earl's steward; Isaac Johnson and John Humphrey were his sons-in-law. Another group of Puritan gentry led by Robert Rich, second Earl of Warwick, was simultaneously planning a colony for Providence Island in the Caribbean.—Ed.

create "the Adventurers of Corporation upon the Place," for the purpose the wording was later made to serve, then such of the leaders as arranged the matter consciously hoodwinked both the government and many of their own associates.

At length, however, the consent of the patentees was obtained, after their counsel had approved the legality of the step; and in October, in contemplation of the removal of the government to America, Winthrop was elected Governor, and Humphrey, Deputy, in place of those who were to remain behind. Eight months later, in the early summer of 1630, Winthrop and a band of between nine hundred and a thousand immigrants landed in America, and settled what were later known as the towns of Charlestown, Boston, Medford, Watertown, Roxbury, Lynn, and Dorchester. Eighty of the inhabitants already planted at Salem under Endicott had died during the winter, and of those who formed the present settlements, about two hundred succumbed between the time of leaving England and the end of December, including Johnson, his wife the Lady Arbella, the Reverend Mr. Higginson, and other important members of the colony.

The settlers, apparently, did not have time to house themselves properly before winter came on, and many, particularly of the poor, had to face the icy winds of a New England January with no better shelter than a canvas tent. Provisions, even in England, were exceedingly scarce and dear that year, partly, some claimed, because of the large quantities taken out by emigrants to New England and the other plantations. Massachusetts had evidently not received her share, if such had been the case, and famine soon faced the settlers, who were forced to live partly on mussels and acorns. Even upon their arrival in the summer, food had been so scarce that they had been forced to give their liberty to a hundred and eighty servants, entailing a loss of between three and four hundred pounds. The cold, which had held off until December 24, suddenly came on in extreme severity, and "such a Christmas eve they had never seen before." The contrast with the Christmas Day which the Warwick settlers were passing at Providence, in the Caribbean, was complete; and Humphrey and Downing, who were in frequent conference with the earl and with Rich, kept writing to advise Winthrop to move the colony farther south, if only to the Hudson River. At a critical moment, the ship Lion, which Winthrop had had the foresight to send at once to England for provisions, arrived with a new supply; but so deep was the discouragement, that many returned in her to the old home, never to come back. Others, however, were of sterner stuff, and took passage in the same boat to fetch their families.

At last the winter passed, and with the summer came renewed hope. The public business had been temporarily managed by the Assistants only, and the first General Court was not held until October. At that session the charter was violated in an important point, in that the freemen relinquished their right to elect the governor and the deputy. Thereafter, it was ruled, these were to be elected by the Assistants only, with whom they were to have the power of making laws and appointing officers. The extent of this limitation of the right of election, which was revoked, however, at the next General Court, is evident from the fact that in March, in contemplation of the probability of there being less than nine Assistants left in the colony, it was agreed that seven should constitute a court. In fact, the charter was continually violated in that regard, as the number of Assistants, for over fifty years, was never more than about one half of the required eighteen.

The Assistants, into whose hands the control of the government now passed, were probably a majority of the entire voting population of the colony. According to the terms of the charter only members of the Company, or the so-called freemen, had the right to vote at its meetings. After the "sea-change" which was presumed to have altered that document into "something rich and strange" in the way of political constitutions, those meetings became the political assemblies of the colony, and the freemen of the Company became the only enfranchised voters of the state. While two thousand persons were settled in Massachusetts about the time of that October meeting, it is probable that not more than sixteen to twenty members of the Company had crossed the ocean, of whom a number had returned or died. If the charter were indeed the written constitution of a state, it was unique among such instruments in that it thus limited all political rights, in a community of two thousand persons, to a tiny self-perpetuating oligarchical group of not more than a dozen citizens. Ninety-nine and one half per cent of the population was thus unenfranchised and unrepresented, and even denied the right of appeal to the higher authorities in England.

Such was the situation, brought about with full knowledge and intention, and as long as possible persisted in, by the Puritan leaders. Those leaders, as we have such clear proof in the case of the noblest of them, John Winthrop, seem to have come to Massachusetts with three distinct and clearly understood objects. They wished, first, to found and develop a peculiar type of community, best expressed by the term Bible-Commonwealth, in which the political and religious elements, in themselves and in their relations to one another, should be but two aspects of the same method of so regulating the lives of individuals as to bring them into harmony with the expressed will of God, as interpreted by the self-appointed rulers. Secondly, both as religious zealots, who felt that they had come into possession of ultimate truth, and as active-minded Englishmen, desirous of an outlet for their administrative energies, they considered themselves as the best qualified rulers and the appointed guardians for the community which they had founded. Lastly, having been largely determined by economic considerations in venturing their fortunes in the enterprise, they looked with fear, as well as jealousy, upon any possibility of allowing control of policy, of law and order, and of legislation concerning person and property, to pass to others.

In such a church-state, no civil question could be considered aside from its possible religious bearings; no religious opinion could be discussed apart from its political implications. It was a system which could be maintained permanently only by the most rigid denial of political free speech and religious toleration. . . . The attitude of the two most influential Massachusetts leaders, lay and ecclesiastical, is not a matter of inference. "Democracy," wrote Winthrop, after stating that there "was no such government in Israel," is "amongst civil nations, accounted the meanest and worst of all forms of government." To allow it in Massachusetts would be "a manifest breach of the 5th. Commandment." "Democracy," wrote John Cotton to Lord Say and Sele, "I do not conceive that ever God did ordeyne as a fit government eyther for church or commonwealth. If the people be governors who shall be governed?"... The democracy of Massachusetts, slow in developing, was the child of the church-covenant and of the frontier, not of the Puritan leaders.

While the latter were thus attempting to found and maintain an aristocracy or oligarchy to guard a church polity which was unconsciously but implicitly democratic, their position was rendered precarious at the very outset, and increasingly so as time went on, by the necessary presence in the colony of that large unenfranchised class which was not in sympathy with them. As we have seen, even under strong social and political temptation, three quarters of the population, though probably largely Puritan in sentiment and belief, persistently refused to ally themselves with the New England type of Puritan church. Their presence in the colony was undoubtedly due to economic motives, more especially, perhaps, the desire to own their lands in fee. It must also have been due to economic considerations on the part of the Puritan rulers. The planting of a Bible-Commonwealth might have been possible without these non-church members, but the creation of a prosperous and populous state was not, as was evidenced by statistics throughout its life. Even of the first thousand who came with Winthrop, it is probable that many were without strong religious motives; that few realized the plans of the leaders; and it is practically certain that the great bulk of them had never seen the charter.

Many of the more active soon wished to have some voice in the management of their own affairs; and at the October meeting of the General Court, one hundred and eight. . .requested that they be made freemen. It became evident to the dozen or so men who alone possessed the governing power, that some extension of the franchise would be necessary if the leading spirits among their two thousand subjects were not to emigrate again to other colonies, or to foment trouble at home. On the other hand, the extension of the franchise was, in their minds, fraught with the perils already indicated. The decision to extend the franchise, but to limit its powers, and to violate the terms of the charter by placing the election of the governor and deputy in the hands of the Assistants instead of the freemen, was probably the result of an effort to solve this problem. Before the next meeting of the General Court in the following May, at which the new freemen were to be admitted, further thought had evidently been devoted to the question, and another solution arrived at. Winthrop was chosen Governor, not by the Assistants, as voted at the preceding meeting, but by "the general consent of the Court, according to the meaning of the patent"; and the momentous resolution was adopted that "noe man shall be admitted to the freedome of this body polliticke, but such as are members of some of the churches within the lymitts of the same." The first attempt on the part of its unenfranchised subjects to secure a larger share of political liberty had resulted merely in establishing, more firmly than before, the theocratical and oligarchical nature of the government.

EDMUND S. MORGAN (1916-), Sterling Professor of History at Yale, was a student of Perry Miller and Samuel Eliot Morison. Sharing their admiration for the Puritans, Morgan has carried on the work of revisionism in his perceptive study of John Winthrop, *The Puritan Dilemma.* In the following selection Morgan describes the political evolution of Massachusetts during the critical years 1630 and 1631. His evaluation of Winthrop's role is especially significant. Morgan explains Winthrop's political ideas by reference to the "covenant theology" he shared with other Puritans. Morgan has depicted Winthrop as a deeply pious layman who came to New England for religious reasons.*

The Massachusetts Bay Company and the People

When Winthrop and eleven other members of the Massachusetts Bay Company met at Cambridge, England, on August 26, 1629, they agreed to go to New England if the charter and headquarters of the company could be transferred with them. Ten of the twelve kept their pledge, eight of them arriving with Winthrop or shortly after. Besides these, Winthrop could count only four or five other members of the company in New England at the end of 1630. This handful of men was now the Massachusetts Bay Company and endowed with all the powers described in the charter which Winthrop guarded among his papers.

In the charter the King had granted authority "to make, ordeine, and establishe all manner of wholesome and reasonable orders, lawes, statutes, and ordinances, directions, and instructions, not contrarie to the lawes of this our realm of England, as well for setling of the forms and ceremonies of government and magistracy fitt and necessary for the said plantation, and the inhabitants there, and for nameing and stiling of all sortes of officers, both superior and inferior, which they shall finde neede-ful for that governement and plantation, and the distinguishing and setting forth of the severall duties, powers, and lymytts of every such office and place."

It was intended, of course, that these extensive powers should be exercised by a

*Reprinted from *The Puritan Dilemma: The Story of John Winthrop* by Edmund S. Morgan (Boston: Little Brown & Company), pp. 84-95. Copyright 1958 by Edmund S. Morgan.

corporation meeting in England; but the charter did not say so, and the only actual limitation which the King placed on the company's governmental authority over Massachusetts Bay was that it should make no laws repugnant to the laws of England. Settlers going to the colony from England and their children born there were to enjoy "all liberties and immunities" that they would have had if they had been born in England. But English birth did not in 1630 confer the right to participate in government, and the charter did not specify that the consent of the settlers should be obtained for the laws made to govern them. Instead the company had full powers to legislate for the colony and to organize a government to carry out their decrees in any way they saw fit.

With regard to the organization and government of the company itself the charter was much more specific. The members, known as "freemen," were to meet four times a year in a "Great and General Court," to make laws for both company and colony. Once a year, at one of these courts, they would elect a governor, a deputy governor, and eighteen "assistants" for the coming year, to manage affairs between meetings of the General Court. This executive council was to meet every month. The governor or deputy governor and at least six of the assistants must be present also at every meeting of the General Court, but the charter did not specify that any other members must be present to constitute a quorum, so that these seven officers, in the absence of any other members, could presumably exercise all the powers of the General Court.

In Massachusetts, therefore, Winthrop and the dozen or so members of the company who came with him had unlimited authority to exercise any kind of government they chose over the other settlers. In order to satisfy the terms of th charter they had only to meet once month as assistants (all but one of th members who are known to have migrate the first year were assistants) and fou times a year as a General Court, thoug the two types of meeting would now b virtually indistinguishable in membership Provided they followed this procedure an passed no laws repugnant to the laws o England, they could govern Massachusett in any way they saw fit. And for tha matter, who was to say what law was re pugnant to those of England? Who was t decide, who to correct them if they erred Here was no King, Parliament, bishop, o judge to stand in their way.

A group of men as sure of their cause a were Winthrop and his friends must hav been strongly tempted to establish themselves as a permanent aristocracy or oligarchy, holding fast the power granted i the charter and using it to enforce th special commission which they believe God had given them. They were a determined, stiff-jawed set, quick to anger an slow to laughter, as likely a group of oligarchs as ever assembled. John Endecot and Thomas Dudley, after Winthrop th most influential of the group, were also th most headstrong.

Endecott had been governing th colony under instructions from th company in England before Winthrop an the others got there. Winthrop saw n need for any such subordinate officer afte his own arrival on the scene, but Endecott was still a member of the company an entitled to a place in its councils. He was a soldier by past experience and by temperament, impatient of civilian impertinence, all too ready to draw his sword or strike out with a fist when his commands were not obeyed with alacrity. The General Court commissioned him to keep the peace in Salem, where he continued to live, but his notion of keeping the peace was sometimes far from peaceful. On one occasion, when a man had not treated him with due respect, he felt obliged to defend his dignity with his fists. When Winthrop rebuked him, he answered, "I acknowledge I was too rash in strikeing him, understanding since that it is not lawfull for a justice of peace to strike. But if you had seene the manner of his carriadge, with such daring of mee with his armes on kembow etc. It would have provoked a very patient man." And this John Endecott was not.

Neither was Thomas Dudley, who as deputy governor was Winthrop's second-in-command. Dudley was a rigid, literal-minded type, ready to exact his pound of flesh whenever he thought it due him. As steward of the Earl of Lincoln in England he had prided himself on getting the Earl out of debt by raising the tenants' rents. In Massachusetts he engrossed quantities of corn and lent it to his poorer neighbors on credit, to receive ten bushels for seven and a half after harvest. Winthrop regarded this practice as oppressive usury, but Dudley's temper flared when his conduct was questioned in any way. He was obviously not the sort of man to diminish his own authority.

Winthrop himself was more mature than Dudley or Endecott would ever be. His long struggle with his passions had left him master of himself in a way that few men ever achieve. The fire was still there, and if blown up by other men's wrath, it would occasionally burst out, but generally it lay well below the surface, imparting a warmth and power which everyone around him sensed. Winthrop, as he himself realized, had acquired a talent for command. He never grasped for authority as Dudley or Endecott might, but he did not need to: he was the kind of man upon whom authority was inevitably thrust.

These three men, all disposed in their different ways to command those around them, were equipped also with a philosophy of government to give their commands a superhuman sanction. For more than a hundred years Protestants had been confronting the pope with declarations of the God-given authority of civil rulers. In England Anglican and Puritan alike maintained the divine right of their king against the enemy at Rome, who claimed a power to depose Protestant monarchs. Though the Puritans reserved to the people a right of resistance against tyrants who violated the laws of God, they were always ready to quote the Epistle to the Romans in support of rulers who enforced the laws of God. And the members of the Massachusetts Bay Company were all godly men; they had come with no other intention than to see God's will done at last.

Winthrop never lost an opportunity to affirm his belief that the powers that be were ordained of God and must be honored and respected accordingly. While still aboard the *Arbella*, he had reminded the other passengers that "God Almightie in his most holy and wise providence hath soe disposed of the Condicion of mankinde, as in all times some must be rich some poore, some highe and eminent in power and dignitie; others meane and in subjeccion." There was no doubt in Winthrop's mind that God intended civil governments to be in the hands of men like himself; to entrust the people at large with powers of government, as in a Greek democracy, was not only unwarranted by Scripture but dangerous to the peace and well-being of the community, for the people at large were unfit to rule. The best part of them was always the smallest part, "and of that best part the wiser part is always the lesser."

Winthrop and the other members of the Bay Company were authorized by their charter to exercise absolute powers of government; they were endowed by temperament with the inclination to exercise those powers; and they were assisted by a philosophy of government which clothed every civil ruler in the armor of divine authority. How natural, then, that they should become a ruling oligarchy. They might readily have succumbed to the lust for power, since power lay unchallenged in their hands.

But they did not succumb.

They did not even keep the powers to which the charter entitled them.

After Winthrop had explored the bay and moved the headquarters of the colony from Salem to Charlestown, he summoned the assistants for their first meeting on August 23, 1630. There were seven members present besides himself and Dudley, and they got down to the business of government at once. They provided for the maintenance of two ministers, set maximum wages for workmen in various trades, and appointed a beadle "to attend upon the Governor, and alwaies to be ready to execute his commands in publique business." They also ordered that there should be regular meetings, or "courts," of the assistants and of the General Court, though the difference between the two would be a formality, since their membership would be virtually identical (unless future emigration brought over other company members without the status of assistant). On September 7 and September 28 they met again as assistants and exercised their authority in a variety of actions. They forbade the sale of firearms to the Indians; they put an embargo on corn; they seized Richard Clough's strong water because he sold too much of it to other men's servants; and they fined Sir Richard Saltonstall, one of their own number, for being absent from court.

Then on October 19 Winthrop summoned at Charlestown the first meeting labeled in the records as a General Court. For this day he and the seven company members who met with him had prepared a revolution that was to affect the history of Massachusetts from that time forward. The records described the event with tantalizing brevity: "For the establishinge of the government. It was propounded if it were not the best course that the Freemen should have the power of chuseing Assistants when there are to be chosen, and the Assistants from amongst themselves to chuse a Governor and Deputy Governor, whoe with the Assistants should have the power of makeing lawes and chuseing officers to execute the same."

This was surely a strange proposal to make to a group of men all of whom were both freemen and assistants. Why, when there were no freemen but themselves in the colony, should they make provision for freemen electing the assistants and the assistants electing the other officers? One begins to get an inkling of what was happening in the next sentence of the records: "This was fully assented unto by the generall vote of the people, and ereccion of hands."

The "people" here referred to were not simply the eight company members present. This we can conclude from events that followed. Winthrop had apparently thrown open the first meeting of the General Court to the whole body of settlers assembled at Charlestown. Together they had established the first constitution of Massachusetts. It used the terminology of the charter, and presumably allowed the provisions of the charter not expressly revised to remain in effect. But by general vote of the people of Massachusetts, the assistants were transformed from an executive council into a legislative assembly; and the term "freeman" was transformed from a designation for the members of a commercial company, exercising legislative and judicial control over that company and its property, into a designation for the citizens of a state, with the right to vote and hold office. The right of the citizen freemen to vote, however, was confined to electing assistants. These assistants, and not the freemen themselves, were to make laws and appoint from their own number a governor and deputy governor.

This transformation of the Bay Company's charter into a constitution for government of the colony would scarcely have been necessary or desirable if the members of the company had intended to keep control in their own hands. The reduction of the freemen's role in the government and the securing of popular consent to this change presaged the admission to freemanship of a large proportion of settlers, men who could contribute to the joint stock nothing but godliness and good citizenship. The transformation of trading company into commonwealth was completed at the next meeting of the General Court, when one hundred and sixteen persons were admitted as freemen. (This was probably most, if not all, of the adult males, excluding servants, then in the colony.) The new freemen then voted that elections should be annual and, doubtless at the behest of Winthrop, that "for time to come noe man shalbe admitted to the freedome of this body pollitické, but such as are members of some of the churches within the lymitts of the same." Though stated in the form of a limitation, this declaration was in fact an open invitation to every future church member in Massachusetts to take up the privileges of freemanship.

Since the people had no political rights under the charter, Winthrop had given them a role to which they had had no legal claim at all. That he confined the gift to church members was not surprising: he would scarcely have wished to take into partnership all of the multitude of men who might come to his colony for the wrong reasons, and the qualified franchise might also help attract the right kind of settlers. By limiting freemanship to church members he extended political rights to a larger proportion of the people than enjoyed such rights in England—and to people who were better qualified to use them than the mere possessors of a forty-shilling freehold. The question that needs to be answered is not why he limited suffrage but why he extended it. What induced Winthrop and the other members of the Bay Company to resign voluntarily the exclusive powers which the charter conferred on them and which their political beliefs and native dispositions made congenial?

Possibly they gave way to popular demand. Possibly they felt a need to keep their own ranks filled. With sickness and death whittling away at their number, they were already close to the minimum quota of seven assistants required by the charter for the holding of the Assistants Court (only six were required in the General Court). But granting their need to perpetuate themselves, they could still have filled vacancies with a few hand-picked men as the need arose. The charter gave them express permission to admit new members to the company if they chose, but it put them under no obligation to do so. Even a popular demand, if it existed, could have been met by a less drastic measure than the one they took.

The real answer as to why they opened the door to freemanship so wide is to be found in the terms of the commission with which they believed the colony was entrusted. The idea of a "covenant," or contract, between God and man occupied a pre-eminent place in their thought: it was the basis of an individual's salvation; it was the origin of every true church and also of every state. "It is of the nature and essence of every society," Winthrop once wrote, "to be knitt together by some Covenant, either expressed or implyed." God's special commission to Massachusetts was an implied covenant.

But there was more than one covenant involved in the establishment of any society. After the people joined in covenant with God, agreeing to be bound by his laws, they must establish a government to see those laws enforced, for they did not have enough virtue to carry out their agreement without the compulsive force of government. They must decide among themselves what form of government they wanted and then create it by a voluntary joint compact—a second covenant.

Winthrop evidently thought that the mere act of coming to Massachusetts constituted a sufficient acceptance of the basic covenant, the special commission which God had given the colony. But the second covenant, establishing the government, required a more explicit agreement. Though the King's charter gave the Bay Company a clear and exclusive right to govern the territory, the King's authority was insufficient. The "due form of government" which Winthrop believed the special commission called for could originate only from a covenant between the settlers and the men who were to rule them. Hence the extraordinary action of October 19, with its sequel, the extension of freemanship.

Winthrop did not believe that in extending freemanship he had transformed Massachusetts into a democracy. The legislative power was lodged not in the people but in a select group where, according to his reading of the Bible, it belonged. Nor was Winthrop's action in securing the consent of the people to his government an affirmation of the principle that governments derive their just powers from the consent of the governed. He did not believe that the officers chosen under the new system would be simply the agents of the people who elected them. Rulers, however selected, received their authority from God, not from the people, and were accountable to God, not to the people. Their business was to enforce the nation's covenant with God, and during their term of office, so long as they devoted themselves to this business, they were free to act as they thought best, suiting their actions to the circumstances.

Winthrop did believe that the people, or a properly qualified portion of them, were entitled to determine the form of government to be established over them and to select the persons who should run that government. These two operations performed, their role was played out until, under the form of government they had chosen, it was time to elect new rulers. If a ruler failed in his duty to enforce the laws of God, the people would be obliged to turn him out without waiting for election time. But so long as he did his duty, his authority was absolute, and, regardless of any errors of judgment he might make, the people were obliged to submit. Indeed, anything less than submission would be rebellion against the authority of God.

In Winthrop's view, then, he had not in any way limited or reduced the authority of government by extending to church members a voice in the selection of the men who were to exercise the authority. Rather he had given to government a practical strength which it could not otherwise have possessed, for Winthrop was enough of a politician to know that, regardless of any divine authority a ruler might claim, people would submit to him more readily if they had a voice in choosing him, especially a Puritan people well educated by their ministers in the principle of government based on covenant.

The struggle of Progressive politicians against the forces of plutocracy inspired VERNON L. PARRINGTON (1871-1929) to analyze American history in terms of a continuous conflict between defenders and opponents of democracy. In his comprehensive study of the American past, *Main Currents in American Thought,* Parrington divides American thinkers into these two camps. Among the Puritans, he discovered a spokesman for democracy in Roger Williams, but he found that John Winthrop and John Cotton opposed any liberalization. Following James Truslow Adams, Parrington describes Cotton and Winthrop as leaders of a theocratic oligarchy. He also argues that Calvin and the Bible were the two most significant influences on the thought of John Cotton. *

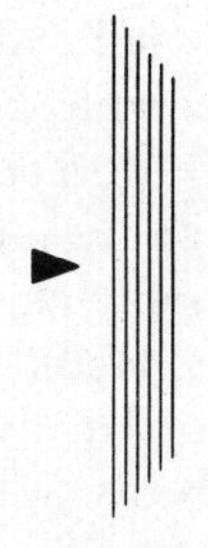

Puritanism as an Antidemocratic Ideology

The most authoritative representative in New England of the ideal of priestly stewardship was the excellent John Cotton, first teacher to the church at Boston. While pastor of the church of St. Botolph, in old Boston, he had dreamed of a Utopia of the Saints, unharassed by tyrannous prelates; and while sweetening his mouth with a morsel of Calvin, as he was fond of doing, no doubt he turned over in his mind the plans and specifications of the Utopia. "When God wrappes us in his ordinances," he said in his sermon to Winthrop's company on the eve of its departure from England, "and warmes us with the life and power of them as with wings, there is the land of Promise." Left behind by the departing brethren, he lingered for a while in an England that was every day becoming colder for such as dreamed of other Canaans than Laud's, until urged by many invitations, at the age of forty-six he followed overseas to devote his remaining life to the great work being done there. For more than a score of years he labored faithfully, and the New England which the emigrant generation bequeathed to its sons bore upon it the marks of John Cotton's shaping hand more clearly than those of any other minister.

It is not easy today to judge fairly the life and work of John Cotton. No adequate

---

*From *Main Currents in American Thought,* Volume I, copyright, 1927, 1930, by Harcourt, Brace & World, Inc.; renewed, 1955, by Vernon L. Parrington, Jr., Louise P. Tucker, Elizabeth P. Thomas. Reprinted by permission of the publishers. Some footnotes omitted.

biography has been written, and his dreams and aspirations lie forgotten in the grave of lost causes and forsaken faiths. But to the Boston freemen of his own day, Master John Cotton was a very great man. Of excellent family and sound university training, he was both a notable theologian and a courteous gentleman. "Twelve hours in a day he commonly studied, and would call that a *scholar's* day," his grandson reported of him. From the hour when he entered Trinity College, Cambridge, at the age of thirteen, to his death in 1652, he was a bookman, and in sheer bulk of acquisition probably no man of his time outdid him. In Cotton Mather's judgment he was "a most *universal scholar*, and a *living system* of the liberal arts, and a *walking library*." His intellectual equipment was so highly regarded that many excellent persons "believed that God would not suffer Mr. Cotton to err"; and that "if ever there be any considerable blow given to the Devil's kingdom," Master Cotton was the man for the business. No other New England champion was so renowned for "beating out the truth in controversie"; and when he turned to the work of answering Roger Williams, the latter exclaimed: "I rejoice it hath pleased [God] to appoint so able, and excellent, and conscionable an Instrument to bolt the Truth to the bran." But though he was bred in Elizabethan days and entered college in the year when Shakespeare's *Henry IV* and Jonson's *Every Man in his Humour* first appeared on the stage, there is no touch of Renaissance splendor in his crabbed style and ascetic reasoning. That was early washed out of him by the rising tide of Hebraism which was slowly submerging the England of poets and playwrights.

But however much he loved cloistered scholarship, the immediate source of his great influence was the spoken rather than the written word. By the universal testimony of his generation he was "a soul-melting preacher," whose reasoned eloquence swayed congregations trained to solid argumentative discourse. When he ascended the pulpit on Sundays and lecture days, he spoke as a prophet in Israel; and on occasions of public ceremonial, or when dissensions arose touching the polity of church or state, he was summoned by the magistrates to convince with his logic and persuade with his eloquence. The strong-minded Anne Hutchinson was but one of many who chose exile in New England rather than lose the edification of Mr. Cotton's preaching. Good men were drawn to him by his sweetness of temper, and evil men were overawed by his venerable aspect. He seems to have been an altogether lovable person, with white hair framing a face that must have been nobly chiseled, gentle-voiced, courteous, tactful, by nature "a tolerant man" who placidly bore with a dissentient and gladly discovered a friend in an antagonist. If this quiet yielding before opposition suggests that he may have been given to opportunism, or his fondness for intellectual subtleties drew from his grandson the comment "a most excellent casuist," we must not too hastily conclude that he served the cause of truth less devotedly than the cause of party.

For a score of years before his coming over, his position in the rising Puritan party had been honorable. Few among the dissenting ministers were better known, none more esteemed. He had shone as an intellectual light at the university, he had long been pastor of one of the loveliest churches in England, he counted among his friends some of the ablest contemporary Englishmen. To Cromwell he was one "whom I love and honour in the Lord"; to Lord Say and Sele, to the Earl of

Warwick, the Earl of Lincoln, and a notable company of Puritan gentlemen, he was a trusted friend and lieutenant; to thousands of the substantial burgesses who were drawing together to form the new Puritan-Whig party, he was "a fixed and conscionable light." That such a leader should have been received with thanksgiving by the Boston congregation was to be expected; that he should have taken high place at once among the members of the Massachusetts oligarchy was equally to be expected. Thenceforth his busy career was no more than a reflection of the ambitions of the theocracy.

Unfortunately his daily contact with narrow-minded and intolerant men gave an unhappy bias to his later career. Cotton seems to have been something of a Puritan intellectual, with an open-minded curiosity that made him receptive to new ideas and tempted him to play with doctrines that were intolerable to his bigoted associates. It was possibly this native sympathy with free speculation that drew him into the camp of Mistress Hutchinson with her doctrine of the inner light. When the schism became serious, dividing the commonwealth into warring camps, Cotton seems to have become frightened and broke with the Boston Antinomians. In this matter he came near to being a shuffler. The Hutchinson trial with its resulting banishments was the turning point of his career in America as it was a crisis in the history of early New England. He was not a man to persecute and harry, nor was he one to stand in isolated opposition to associates whom he respected, and he allowed himself to be coerced by narrower-minded men like Endicott and Dudley. After 1637 the better nature of John Cotton was submerged by the rising intolerance, and "the most tolerant, as he was the ablest of the Massachusetts divines," was brought so low as to defend the meanest and cruelest acts of the oligarchy. He descended to disgraceful casuistry in defense of the first whippings of the Quakers, and he urged the death penalty upon King Philip's son and the enslavement of the remnant of Philip's tribe, against the plea of John Eliot that "to sell soules for mony seemeth to me a dangerous merchandize." The sins of the oligarchy rest in large measure on the head of John Cotton, and the judgment of the most recent historian of New England must stand:

> With a broader mind and wider vision than any of the other clergy of the colony, he had not the courage to stand alone, beyond a certain point, against their unanimity in intolerance. The higher promptings of his nature were crushed by the united voice of the priesthood, as Winthrop's had been so short a time before, and the noblest of the colony's leaders, lay and clerical, from that time tended to sink to the lower level of their fellows.[1]

An apologist—and whoever has felt the charm of John Cotton's personality easily becomes an apologist—will perhaps find some grounds of excuse for his later conduct. He was in an unhappy position. He was ill at ease in his mind, and his frequent tacking in the face of adverse winds was characteristic of the intellectual who sees all sides of a question. He heartily approved of the theocratic ends that his associates were seeking, and his influential position made him the defender of acts which his better nature must have disapproved. The historian, however, will seek a more adequate explanation in the roots of his environment. The idealism of John Cotton was the fruit of his training, and his theocratic dreams were conditioned by the facts that he was both a Calvinist and a Carolinian gentleman. The fusion of these two influences resulted in the unique politi-

[1] James Truslow Adams, *The Founding of New England*, p. 170.

cal theory of an ethical aristocracy, consecrated to moral stewardship in the state. A lifelong student of Calvin's *Institutes,* he found there a system of social organization that responded to every demand of the theologian and the aristocrat. The very texture and pattern of Cotton's political philosophy is exemplified in such a passage as this, over which he must have brooded much:

> When these three forms of government of which philosophers treat, are considered in themselves, I, for my part, am far from denying that the form which greatly surpasses the other is aristocracy, either pure or modified by popular government; not indeed in itself, but because it very rarely happens that kings so rule themselves as never to dissent from what is just and right, or are possessed of so much acuteness and prudence as always to see correctly. Owing therefore to the vices or defects of men, it is safer and more tolerable when several bear rule, that they may thus mutually assist, instruct, and admonish each other, and should any be disposed to go too far, the others are censors and masters to curb his excess. This has already been proved by experience, and confirmed also by the authority of the Lord himself, when he established an aristocracy bordering on popular government among the Israelites, keeping them under that as the best form, until He exhibited an image of the Messiah in David.

As a Carolinian gentleman, this was as far as Cotton would go on the path of liberalism. The elders were responsible to God for the spiritual well-being of the people, and the state must aid and not hinder them in their leadership. The doctrine of unlimited popular sovereignty was for him no other than a thistle in the garden of the Lord. The desire for liberty he regarded as the sinful prompting of the natural man, a denial of the righteous authority of God's chosen rulers. If democracy were indeed the best form of government, was it not strange that divine wisdom should have failed to discover the fact? In the history of the chosen people nowhere does God approve the democratic as the best form, but the theocratic; was He now to be set right by sinful men who courted popularity by appealing to the selfishness of depraved hearts? To the scripturist the logic of his argument was convincing:

> It is better that the commonwealth be fashioned to the setting forth of God's house, which is his church: than to accommodate the church frame to the civill state. Democracy, I do not conceyve that ever God did ordeyne as a fit government eyther for church or commonwealth. If the people be governors, who shall be governed? As for monarchy, and aristocracy, they are both of them clearly approoved, and directed in scripture, yet so as referreth the soveraigntie to himselfe, and setteth up Theocracy in both, as the best forme of government in the commonwealth, as well as in the church.

If John Cotton, like other Carolinian gentlemen, was a confirmed aristocrat, he was at the same time a social revolutionary, who would substitute an aristocracy of the Saints for the landed aristocracy, and refashion society upon ethical rather than economic lines. At what time the ideal of a Presbyterian Bible commonwealth took shape in his mind, it is impossible to determine; but it was a natural outcome of his most cherished beliefs. A devout scripturist, he accepted the Bible as a rule of universal application, perfect and final. The sufficiency of the Scriptures to all social needs was axiomatic with him; "the more any law smells of man the more unprofitable," he asserted in his draft of laws offered for acceptance by the commonwealth; and at another time he exclaimed, "*Scripturae plenitudinem adoro.*" He chose exile rather than yield to what he regarded as the unscriptural practices of Laud, and now that he was come to a new land where a fresh beginning was to be made, was it not his Christian duty to "endeavour after a *theocracy*, as near as might be, to that which was the glory of Israel, the 'peculiar people' "? The old Common Law must be superseded by the Mosaic dispensation; the citizen of the commonwealth must become the subject of Jehovah; the sovereignty of temporal authorities must serve the higher sovereignty of God.

Holding to such views the duty devolving upon him was plain: to assist the magistrates in checking the dangerous drift towards a democratic organization of church and state, which the new environment encouraged; and to defend the theocratic ideal against all critics. The first he sought to accomplish by creating a more perfect theocratic machinery. As we catch glimpses of him moving tactfully back and forth through the brisk little scenes, he seems always to have a finger in some magisterial affair. Three months after his arrival in Boston he preached a sermon, the purport of which Winthrop noted in his *Journal*:

> After much deliberation and serious advice the Lord directed the teacher Mr. Cotton, to make clear by the scripture, that the minister's maintenance, as well as all other charges of the church, should be defrayed out of a stock, or treasury, which was to be raised out of the weekly contribution: which accordingly was agreed upon.

In his first election sermon, preached in the May following, he joined issue with the democratic spirit of the deputies, by supporting a principle which was flagrantly oligarchical:

> That a magistrate ought not to be turned into the condition of a private man without just cause, & to be publicly convict, no more than the magistrates may turn a private man out of his freehold, etc., without like public trial, etc.

Unrebuffed by the rejection of this curious doctrine of the freehold tenure of magistrates, Cotton made a more ambitious attempt to theocratize the state, when at the October court of 1636, in response to the persistent pressure for a fundamental law, he presented his code for adoption by the commonwealth, the scriptural origin of which is revealed in the title, "Model of Moses his Judicials." Cotton Mather tells of this venture in constitution making, in the following glowing but inaccurate words:

> On Mr. Cotton's arrival he found the whole country in a perplexed & a divided state, as to their *civill constitution*. . . . It was then requested of Mr. *Cotton* that he would, from the laws wherewith God governed his ancient people, form an *abstract* of such as were of a moral and a lasting equity; which he performed as acceptably as judiciously. But inasmuch as very much of an *Athenian democracy* was in the mould of the government, by the royal charter. . . . Mr. Cotton effectually recommended it unto them that none should be *electors*, nor *elected* therein, except such as were *visible subjects* of our Lord Jesus Christ, personally *confederated* in our churches. In these, and many other ways, he propounded unto them an endeavor after a theocracy, as near as might be, to that which was the glory of Israel, the "peculiar people."

Cotton's code was rejected in favor of one, somewhat less Hebraic, prepared by Nathaniel Ward, but he continued to be the chief guide and mentor to the magistrates in political as well as theological matters, and his theocratic philosophy determined in large measure the policy of the oligarchy. To found an Hebraic state in which political rights should be subordinate to religious conformity, in which the magistrates should be chosen from a narrow group, with authority beyond the reach of the popular will, and with the ministers serving as court of last resort to interpret the divine law to the citizen-subjects of Jehovah—this was the great ambition of John Cotton; and the untiring zeal and learned scriptural authority which he dedicated to that ambition justify us in regarding him as the greatest of the New England theocrats. In the categories of the Puritan philosophy of ethical stewardship there was no recognition of the profane doctrine of natural rights. Freedom was the prerogative of righteousness; the well-being of society required that the sinner should remain subject to the Saint. Nowhere does he lay down this principle more unmistakably than in an important state paper:

> Now if it be a divine truth, that none are to be trusted with public permanent authority but godly men, who are fit materials for church membership, then from the same grounds it will appear, that none are so fit to be trusted with the liberties of the commonwealth as church members. For, the liberties of this commonwealth are such, as require men of faithful integrity to God and the state, to preserve the same. . . . Now. . .these liberties are such as carry along much power with them, either to establish or subvert the commonwealth, and therewith the church, which power, if it be committed to men according to their godliness. . .then, in case worldly men should prove the major part, as soon they might do, they would readily set over us magistrates like themselves, such as might. . .turn the edge of all authority and laws against the church and the members thereof, the maintenance of whose peace is the chief end which God aimed at in the institution of magistracy.

This, quite evidently, is the negation of democracy, and it has been freely charged against his reputation by later critics. But in fairness it must be added, that it is equally the negation of the principle of hereditary aristocracy; and to reject the latter was a severer test of his integrity then to deny the former. He wanted neither a democracy nor an aristocracy to control the church-state. "Hereditary honors both nature and scripture doth acknowledge," he argued cautiously in reply to "Certain Proposals made by Lord Say, Lord Brooks, and other Persons of quality, as conditions of their removing to New-England." "Two distinct ranks we willingly acknowledge. . .the one of them called Princes, or Nobles, or Elders (amongst whom gentlemen have their place), the other the people." To the former he willingly accorded the right of rulership so long as they were of approved godliness, faithful to their stewardship. But "if God should not delight to furnish some of their posterity with gifts fit for magistracy, we should expose them rather to reproach and prejudice, and the commonwealth with them, than exalt them to honor, if we should call them forth, when God doth not, to public authority." It must be set down in John Cotton's accounts that he discouraged the transplanting of English aristocracy to the soil of Massachusetts.

B. KATHERINE BROWN shares with her husband, the historian Robert E. Brown, an interest in the evolution of democracy during the colonial period. In studies of the number of eligible voters in eighteenth-century Massachusetts and Virginia, the Browns strongly challenge the traditional assumption that colonial governments were completely in the hands of the aristocracy. Mrs. Brown reaches similar conclusions about Massachusetts when it was supposedly an oligarchic state ruled over by Winthrop and Cotton. Her argument with Parrington and James Truslow Adams is based on the meaning of the words aristocracy and democracy in Puritan political theory. She finds their meaning then, quite different from their meaning now.*

The Puritan Concept of Aristocracy

"Aristocracy" and "democracy," as words descriptive of the political structure of society, present problems to writers on American history because of the difficulty of definition. What assurance is there, for example, that writers of seventeenth-century Massachusetts, writing of "aristocracy" and "democracy," were thinking in the same terms as later historians who use the words in describing this same seventeenth-century society? Today "aristocracy" and "democracy" are recognized as contrasting types of governments. In an aristocracy, the state is governed and the laws are made by a small privileged class which is not elected by the people and which retains power either by custom, or by force, or by heredity. On the other hand, a democracy is a government in which the supreme power is retained by the people and generally exercised indirectly by their representatives. Although the governing power, the electorate, may be a minority of the total population—as in the United States, especially before woman suffrage—the principle on which the government is based in a democracy is popular sovereignty. We call it "democracy" when we delegate authority to elected officials to make laws and to

*B. Katherine Brown, "A Note on the Puritan Concept of Aristocracy," *Mississippi Valley Historical Review*, XLI (June 1954), pp. 105-112. Reprinted without the footnotes by permission of the managing editor of *The Journal of American History*.

govern. The writers in seventeenth-century Massachusetts had ideas of their own about the meaning of these words; and in passing judgment on the "aristocratic" or "democratic" character of the political structure of Puritan society, therefore, it appears desirable to inquire further how the words were being used by members of the society itself.

Modern writers are inclined to agree, with Vernon L. Parrington, that in the early Bay Colony there was a "persistent hostility of the leaders to every democratic tendency." Others have emphasized the aristocratic or oligarchic element of the rule of the few. John D. Hicks, in his widely used textbook, wrote that "Early Massachusetts was not a democracy; it was an aristocratic theocracy"; and Thomas J. Wertenbaker described the commonwealth as a government of the many by the few. One thing seems apparent: Modern critics in general do not believe that Puritan society was run by the will of the majority.

One of the frequently cited sources for this modern point of view is the famous statement by John Cotton which condemns democracy as the worst form of government. Writing to Lord Say in 1636, he said: "I do not conceyve that ever God did ordeyne [it] as a fitt government eyther for church or commonwealth." "As for monarchy, and aristocracy," he continued, "they are both of them clearly approved, and directed in scripture, yet so as referreth the soveraigntie to himself, and setteth up Theocracy in both, as the best forms of government in the commonwealth, as well as in the church." Cotton, it would appear, approved of aristocracy as a form of government and explicitly disapproved of democracy. Too much may be inferred from his aristocratic preferences. Too much *is* inferred if his predilection for aristocracy is understood to mean a denial of participation in government by "the people."

What Cotton meant by aristocracy has a close relationship to what we call democracy today. He explained his meaning to Lord Say a few paragraphs later in the same letter:

> Nor neede your Lordship feare (which yet I speake with submission to your Lordships better judgment) that this corse will lay such a foundation, as nothing but mere democracy can be built upon it. Bodine confesseth, that though it be *status popularis*, where a people choose their owne governors; yet the government is not a democracy, if it bė administred, not by the people, but by the governors, whether one (for then it is a monarchy, though elective) or by many, for then (as you know) it is aristocracy. In which respect it is, that church government is justly denyed (even by Mr. Robinson) to be democratical, though the people choose their owne officers and rulers.

In other words, in Cotton's opinion, the people might participate in government, by the exercise of the franchise, whether or not the form of government was democracy, monarchy, or aristocracy. What distinguished these forms of government was the identity of the governing agent: in democracy, the people; in monarchy, an individual; in aristocracy, a group of individuals. Cotton defined aristocracy by how many ruled, not by how those rulers came to power. If the people governed, it was democracy; if the delegates chosen by the people governed, it was aristocracy. There was more than an academic similarity between Cotton's "aristocracy" and representative democracy.

Cotton, it should be remembered, was not giving this explanation to the Massachusetts freemen to answer their demands for a larger share in the government. He was writing this definition in a private letter to Lord Say and Seal and was obviously trying to overcome this nobleman's fear of too much democracy in the colony. Cotton was hoping that Lord Say would settle there and was arguing that even if the people elected their officers it was not mere democracy and would not lead to political instability. He was underscoring the aristocratic aspects of the Massachusetts government and playing down the democratic tendencies for the benefit of a convincing argument.

In Cotton's other writings he leaves no doubt in the reader's mind that he strongly believed in the liberties of the people, including their right to elect their own rulers. According to John Winthrop, Cotton declared in a sermon preached in 1634 that the strength of the magistracy was their authority, the strength of the people was their liberty, and the strength of the ministry was their purity. All of these should have a negative voice, he said, but the ultimate power ought to be in the whole body of the people. Ten years later he expressed the same view. In his main treatise on church government, he emphasized that a balance of power in government is best, whether in church or commonwealth, and he listed the right to elect their officers as the first power of the people.

John Winthrop, the leading civil spokesman of the time, agreed with Cotton's basic definition of aristocracy. He believed that the people should elect their rulers but those rulers, once chosen, should be obeyed. In his objection to the type of petition sent to the general court in 1639 by some Roxbury freemen, Winthrop did not question the right of the people to choose their leaders but he did resent their resistance to laws not repugnant to the law of God. He believed that once the people had "chosen" their rulers to make their laws they were bound by oath to submit to such laws. For the lesser part of them to combine together in a public petition to repeal any order which was not repugnant to the law of God savored of resisting an ordinance of God. Having deputed authority to others, the people had no power to make or alter laws but were to obey laws made by their elected officials. If any order seemed unlawful or inconvenient, the people should present reasons to the court for their discontent and ask the court to review the questionable act. This arrangement would be much better than "peremptorily to petition to have it repealed, which amounts to plain reproof of those whom God hath set over them, and putting dishonor upon them, against the tenor of the fifth commandment."

Winthrop developed this concept of rulership more completely in 1645 during the dispute which arose in Hingham over choosing a captain for the militia. When Winthrop, the deputy-governor, made a decision against the majority will, eighty-one men of Hingham protested to the general court in a petition and complained against the deputy-governor. He was tried before the general court and finally acquitted, but afterward he declared: "The great questions that have troubled the country, are about the authority of the magistrates and the liberty of the people. It is yourselves who have called us to this office, and being called by you, we have our authority from God, in a way of an ordinance. . . ." And, he continued, "when you choose magistrates, you take them from among yourselves, men subject to like passions as you are. . . . We account him a good servant, who breaks not his covenant. The covenant between you and us is the oath you have taken of us, which is to this purpose, that we shall govern you and judge your causes by the rules of God's laws and our own, according to our best skill." It is obvious that Winthrop did not question the people's right to elect their rulers, but he insisted that once elected those rulers should be obeyed. It must also be remembered that he was saying this at a time when the people were definitely questioning his methods of rule.

Winthrop called the Massachusetts commonwealth of his day a "mixt Aristocratie." And he believed that the people's power of election was the democratic part of the government. He wrote of the democratic element in this commonwealth as follows: "Where the Chief Ordinary power and administration. . .is in the people there is a Democracie," adding that "the Deputyes are the Democraticall parte of our Government," because if the power "be in the Deputyes it is in the people." By implication, at least, he agreed with other early Massachusetts leaders in considering the governor and assistants as the aristocratic element in this "mixt Aristocratie."

To understand how the deputies came to be considered the democratic part of the government while the governor and assistants were considered the aristocratic part, it is necessary to trace the development of government in the colony. When the Massachusetts government was first established, in October, 1630, the rule was for the freemen to choose the assistants and the assistants to choose the governor and deputy-governor from among themselves. In 1632 this method was changed and the whole general court—composed of governor, deputy-governor, assistants, and freemen—chose the new governor, deputy-governor, and assistants with the restriction that the governor was always to be chosen from among the assistants. However, two years later as the freemen increased in number, the law was again altered and from that time on the freemen were to elect deputies to represent them and act for them in all matters except elections, in which every freeman was still to voice his opinion. This procedure continued in force until 1647, at which time the freemen ceased to vote in person for governor and assistants at the annual court of elections but sent in their sealed votes from each town to be counted. As a statement of the general court in 1646 put it, the people were "present" in the general court by their deputies; the governor and assistants were the "Aristocraticall" part and the deputies the "Democratticall" part of the court. In other words, the deputies, because they were the direct spokesmen of local areas, of certain groups of people, were considered the democratic element, but the governor and assistants, because they were spokesmen for the colony at large, were considered the aristocratic parts.

Additional evidence that the Massachusetts leaders believed they had a mixed aristocracy, different from what would be understood by "aristocracy" today, is found in a statement by the Massachusetts elders in 1644. They declared that the Massachusetts general court was not a "pure aristocracy, but mixt of an aristocracy & democracy." And, they continued, although the Massachusetts patent made their government "mixt" in the general court, yet it instituted subordinate administrations of justice to be "aristocratically" dispensed by the court of assistants; but even in these courts there was a "democraticall" element in the jury. At this time, the Massachusetts court of assistants acted as judges but the jurors were elected from among and by the freemen.

Like Cotton and Winthrop, other contemporary Massachusetts writers looked upon early Massachusetts as a mixed aristocracy. Thomas Lechford referred to the seventeenth-century commonwealth, in words sounding oddly in contrast today, as a "popular or Aristocraticall government."

Another writer, Edward Johnson, commented, about the year 1650, that the Massachusetts general court consisted "of a mixt company, part Aristocracy, and part Democracy of Magistrates," and later referred to the Massachusetts commonwealth as "our Democracy." Johnson, of course, in this particular passage, was emphasizing the democratic element of the Bay Colony government, just as Cotton had emphasized the aristocratic element in his letter to Lord Say and Seal. But both men were speaking of the same government, a "mixt' Aristocratie" in which the people elected their rulers from among themselves.

In two other aspects—those of wealth and heredity—the Puritan "mixt Aristocratie" is much nearer our notion of democracy than our current meaning of aristocracy. It is customary for us to associate with the word the idea of wealth and usually, also, hereditary right. Neither wealth nor the prescriptive rights of birth was included in the Puritan concept of aristocracy found in Massachusetts. Instead a sense of moral obligation on the part of the rulers was stressed, a factor which has generally been pushed aside in the modern definition of the word.

Cotton and other leading men in the colony clearly opposed the idea of wealth as a basis for freemanship in the formative period of the Bay State. This is shown in a paper returned to Lord Say and Seal in 1636, the same time that Cotton wrote his explanatory letter to the nobleman. Lord Say had proposed that certain conditions concerning the colony's government were necessary before he would come to the colony, and he listed these under ten "demands." Cotton, with the aid of leading magistrates, ministers, and freeholders, answered each demand separately. Among other things, the nobleman demanded that a certain amount of material wealth be the basis for the rank of freeman. "We must confess," answered Cotton and the others, "our ordinary practice to be otherwise." Except the old planters who were admitted freemen before the churches were established in the colony, no one was admitted to freemanship but members of some church in the commonwealth. Of such, none were excluded from the liberty of freemen, but the magistrates were chosen out of the most eminent freemen only. Of those outside the church, the leaders explained, there were some specially endowed with wisdom and a sense of justice; but although they might be safely employed to assist the governors, they were not to be trusted with standing power or settled authority.

The Bay Colony leaders as firmly rejected Lord Say's demand that a hereditary aristocracy be established to which none might be admitted except by the consent of both houses of the general court. The Massachusetts men graciously assured the nobleman that they would consider it a favor from God for him to settle among them and that they would gladly receive not only Lord Say but his friends with honor, for hereditary honors were acknowledged in both nature and scripture. But, they continued, hereditary authority and power comes only from civil law. If God had blessed these gentlemen with gifts for government, it would be a sin to neglect such men in public elections, but if they were not so blessed, it would only expose them to reproach to call them to office when God had not fitted them for such.

In form, then, Puritan aristocracy bears a strong resemblance to our modern democracy. Officials were elected by the people and given authority to rule. They believed, as we do today, that laws once made should be obeyed until those laws were officially changed. And, as in our modern democracy, wealth and heredity carried no weight in government.

There is a philosophical difference, of course, between Puritan aristocracy and modern democracy. The underlying philosophy of the Puritan had a heavy religious tone not found in modern politics. In spite of the fact, as Cotton expressed it, that the ultimate power should be in the people, the Bay Colony leaders, once chosen, were looked upon as the spokesmen of God, and the laws, once made, were a reflection of divine guidance. This religious tone has faded to near nothingness in modern politics. Today our representatives are looked upon as spokesmen of the people and the laws are the reflection of the social and economic fabric of society.

Some may consider, also, that Puritan Massachusetts would still not be a democracy in the modern sense because the franchise was limited to freemen only. Current authorities differ decidedly on this issue. Charles M. Andrews points out that while few could vote in early Massachusetts, all men had some share in government by 1652. Samuel E. Morison, however, believes that most men could vote before 1650, but that after that date church membership fell off sharply. Wertenbaker states that from its inception Puritan government was a government of the many by the few.

This disagreement among authorities highlights the need for a deeper understanding of Puritan society, and failure to determine the contemporary meaning of "aristocracy" has added to the confusion. When we recognize that Puritan aristocracy closely resembles our modern democracy, we may have to reconsider the "persistent hostility" of the Puritan leaders to every democratic tendency.

In 1648 the colony of Massachusetts adopted a comprehensive code of laws. According to the legal historian GEORGE LEE HASKINS (1915-), who is Professor of law at the University of Pennsylvania, the code of 1648 was "the first compilation of its kind in the English-speaking world." For this reason alone the code merits attention; but it is also a significant clue to the intentions of the colonists. Did they carry over to America the legal traditions of England, or did their Puritanism make them legal reformers? Was the Bible the only source of the code, or did it owe something to the English common law? These are questions that Haskins answers in his convincing analysis of the interplay between "tradition" and "design" in the code of 1648.*

The Sources of Law in Massachusetts

"In all their administrations," wrote John Winthrop in defense of the constitutionality of the early Massachusetts government, "the Officers of this Bodye Politick have a Rule to walk by. . .which Rule is the *Worde of God*. . . ." The basic content of that rule, in Puritan eyes, was to be found in the Bible, wherein God had provided an immutable constitution not only, as John Cotton said, "for the right ordering of a private mans soule to everlasting blessednes with himselfe, but also for the right ordering of a mans family, yea, of the commonwealth too, so farre as both of them are subordinate to spiritual ends. . . ."

That the word of God provided the mainspring for the colony mission is hardly open to doubt. The reform and purification of church discipline and doctrine through a return to the principles of the primitive apostolic church was not only the deliberate and unswerving aim of the early Puritans in England but the primary purpose of the founding of the Bay Colony. To God's word as declared in Scripture the colonists consistently turned for guidance and justification, both in matters of church polity and in the framing and administration of their laws. The decisions of the courts were expected to conform to that Word, and an order of the General Court in 1636 had expressly so provided in situations for which no posi-

*Reprinted with permission of The Macmillan Company from *Law and Authority in Early Massachusetts* by George L. Haskins. Copyright George Lee Haskins, 1960. Footnotes omitted.

tive law had been established. Moreover, the Epistle to the Code of 1648 proclaimed that it had been "no small priviledge, and advantage to us in New-England. . .to frame our civil Politie, and lawes according to the rules of [God's] most holy word," and the capital laws therein contained were specifically annotated to chapter and verse of the Old Testament. Several of those provisions, as well as other enactments, incorporated literal biblical phraseology into the body of statutory law.

The colonists' reliance upon biblical precedent and authority, apparent in the pronouncements of their leaders and in the fabric of the legal system, has led some scholars to conclude that the law of early Massachusetts was essentially biblical, and even to characterize the colony as the "Bible Commonwealth." Although such generalizations are not without foundation, their value is lessened by failure to examine them from the standpoint of the law as a whole and with reference both to the special conditions of settlement and to the social, political, and legal inheritance which the Puritans shared in common with other seventeenth century Englishmen.

At the outset, it should be observed that influential as the Bible was in the lives of the colonists, it also held a position of extraordinary importance for their English contemporaries. Recourse to, and reliance upon, the teachings of Scripture was by no means confined to the Puritans and was common throughout England in the sixteenth and seventeenth centuries. By the time of the settlement of Massachusetts, the Bible in English translation had been widely available for nearly a century. Henry VIII had at one point sought to stem developing interest therein through a prohibition against its being read by servants and women; yet the impetus of the English Reformation so stimulated popular demand for free access to the Scriptures that by the 1530's Bible reading was actively encouraged by the Tudor government. In 1538 it was ordered that every parish in the country should purchase a copy of the Bible in English, to be set up in each church, "where the parishioners might most commodiously resort to the same and read it." As the century wore on, the Bible, in cheap and readily available editions, had become the common property of all classes of English society. Children in school were taught to read from books studded with scriptural selections, and by the beginning of the seventeenth century virtually every literate English household had its own copy. The rich imagery of its texts quickened the imagination and left an indelible imprint upon English speech and letters, while its precepts and parables, no longer buried in the obscurities of the Latin tongue or meted out at the discretion of a priestly caste, became a powerful force not only in molding religious ideas but in shaping the everyday conduct of English people in all walks of life. . . .

Hardly less striking was the influence of the Bible upon English law and legal thinking. Belief in the Scriptures as a source of law was widespread among educated Englishmen, partly because of the persisting influence of mediaeval scholasticism and partly because of the tendency of Protestant theologians to equate natural law with Mosaic law. English exiles who had lived at Geneva during the reign of Mary had seen at firsthand a legal system that owed much to biblical precepts, and the influence of Calvinism in Scotland had resulted in the enactment of the eighteenth chapter of Leviticus as the positive law of the northern kingdom. As part of the effort to prove the English Church's claim to apostolic succession, the sixteenth century had seen the publication and widespread praise of the early code of

Alfred the Great, which incorporated the Decalogue and much of four chapters of Exodus as part of the laws of England. Thomas Cromwell, Henry VIII's Chief Minister, had even ordered the reading of the Ten Commandments at the end of every Sabbath service. . . .

Unquestionably, therefore, Englishmen of the sixteenth and seventeenth centuries were thoroughly conversant with the Bible and accustomed to looking upon it as authority. It is equally without question that the influence of the Bible upon conceptions of what the law ought to be was more pronounced and more inclined toward literalism among the English Puritans than among their non-Puritan countrymen. The former saw themselves as children of Israel, openly imitated Hebraic practices, and likened their persecutions to the misery of the Jews at the hands of Antiochus. By the same token, they were convinced that much of the law that God had given to ancient Israel continued to bind the people whom He had chosen as His own in the England of Elizabeth and James. "So soon as God had set up Politicall Government among his people Israel," recites the Epistle to the Code of 1648, "hee gave them a body of lawes for judgement both in civil and criminal causes. These were breif and fundamental principles, yet withall so full and comprehensive as out of them clear deductions were to be drawne to all particular cases in future times." Pursuant to this kind of thinking, Thomas Cartwright, in the time of Elizabeth, had urged the necessity of the death penalty for blasphemers and unruly children; and Puritan reformers of the Interregnum were to employ the same reasoning in pressing for the literal enactment of the Mosaic code.

None of the Massachusetts laws more clearly reflects biblical influence than do the provisions of the capital laws contained in the Code of 1648. Idolatry, witchcraft, blasphemy, bestiality, sodomy, adultery, rape, man stealing, treason, false witness with intent to take life, cursing or smiting of a parent, stubbornness or rebelliousness on the part of a son against his parents, and homicide committed with malice prepense, by guile or poisoning, or "suddenly in. . .anger or cruelty of passion"—all were punishable with death. Each of these provisions, with the exception of that relating to rape, was annotated to some chapter and verse of the Pentateuch, and several exactly reproduced its language. No more striking proof of literal reliance upon the Bible in this area of the law can be found than in the law relating to rebellious sons, which is here quoted in full, to the right of the text of Deuteronomy 21:18—21:

> If a man have a stubborn and rebellious son, which will not obey the voice of his father, or the voice of his mother, and that, when they have chastened him, will not hearken unto them: Then shall his father and his mother lay hold on him, and bring him out unto the elders of his city, and unto the gate of his place; and they shall say unto the elders of his city, This our son is stubborn and rebellious, he will not obey our voice; he is a glutton, and a drunkard. And all the men of his city shall stone him with stones, that he die. . . .
>
> If a man have a stubborn OR REBELLIOUS SON, of sufficient years & understanding (*viz*) sixteen years of age, which will not obey the voice of his Father, or the voice of his Mother, and that when they have chastened him will not harken unto them: then shal his Father & Mother being his natural parents, lay hold on him, & bring him to the Magistrates assembled in Court & testifie unto them, that their Son is stubborn & rebellious & will not obey their voice and chastisement, but lives in sundry notorious crimes, such a son shal be put to death.

Other capital laws contain clauses, phrases, or words taken directly from the Old Testament. Thus, the witchcraft provision defined a witch as one that "hath or consulteth with a familiar spirit" in terms of Leviticus 20:27 and Deuteronomy 18:11, which speak respectively of one "that hath a familiar spirit" and of "a consulter with familiar spirits." Again, it is prescribed in Leviticus 20:15 and 16 that "if a man lie with a beast, he shall surely be put to death: and ye shall slay the beast," and similar punishment was provided "if a woman approach unto any beast, and lie down thereto"; by comparison, the bestiality law of Massachusetts states that "If any man or woman shall LYE WITH ANY BEAST, or bruit creature, by carnall copulation; they shall surely be put to death: and the beast shall be slain, & buried, and not eaten." In the same chapter of Leviticus, 20:13, it is stated that "If a man also lie with mankind, as he lieth with a woman, both of them have committed an abomination"; the colony law against sodomy prescibes that "If any man LYETH WITH MAN-KINDE as he lieth with a woman, both of them have committed abomination. . . ." In Exodus 21:16 it is declared that "he that stealeth a man, and selleth him, or if he be found in his hand, he shall surely be put to death"; in Massachusetts law, "If any man STEALETH A MAN, or Man-kinde, he shall surely be put to death." Finally, the colonial provision that "If any child, or children. . .shall CURSE, or SMITE their natural FATHER, or MOTHER; he or they shall be put to death:" is paralleled by Exodus 21:15 and 17, to the effect that "he that smiteth his father, or his mother. . .And he that curseth his father, or his mother, shall surely be put to death."

At the same time, even those capital laws which are unequivocally based upon the Bible contain evidence of substantial non-Scriptural influences. The sodomy law, for example, is qualified by an exception in favor of one who was "forced (or be under fourteen years of age in which case he shall be severely punished)." This exception demonstrates that in the course of revising an earlier law, first enacted in the Body of Liberties, the colonists not only took account of the element of intent but introduced the recognized English legal presumption that a boy under fourteen years of age was deemed to be legally incapable of committing sodomy. Significantly, legal presumptions based upon age are also apparent in the colony law against cursing or smiting of parents and in that dealing with stubborn and rebellious sons. Those laws, which were originally enacted by the General Court in November, 1646, were made applicable, respectively, to "any child, or children, above sixteen years old, and of sufficient understanding," and to a son "of sufficient years & understanding (*viz*) sixteen years of age." In the former law a second qualification of Scripture was introduced for cases in which "it can be sufficiently testified that the Parents have been very unchristianly negligent in the education of such children; or so provoked them by extream, and cruel correction; that they have been forced therunto to preserve themselves from death or maiming." This qualification appears to represent, as the absolute biblical injunction does not, an effort to accommodate the community's interest in ensuring the observance of God's command that parents be honored with the Puritan view that parents should provide their children with a proper moral and religious education, and should use moderation in correcting them.

Like the sodomy statute, the blasphemy statute was amended in important respects between its original enactment in 1641 and its incorporation into the Code in 1648. The 1648 version is quoted in full, with the additions italicized in order to demonstrate the extent to which the draftsmen consciously applied considered policy to its revision:

If any person *within this Jurisdiction whether Christian or Pagan shall wittingly and willingly presume to* BLASPHEME the *holy* Name of God, Father, Son or Holy-Ghost, with direct, expresse, presumptuous, or highhanded blasphemy, *either by wilfull or obstinate denying the true God, or his Creation, or Government of the world:* or shall curse God in like manner, *or reproach the holy Religion of God as if it were but a politick device to keep ignorant men in awe; or shal utter any other kinde of Blasphemy of the like nature & degree they* shall be put to death.

The first of the three amendments specifically extends the reach of the capital law to the Indians, pursuant to biblical authority afterward cited that "as well the stranger, as he that is born in the land, when he blasphemeth the name of the Lord, shall be put to death." The second, as well as the first amendment, introduces the fundamental Puritan idea of the offender's moral responsibility for a criminal act, based upon his knowing and deliberate choice. Equally important is the third addition, which requires that the offenders be "wilfull or obstinate," and emphasizes the Puritan belief, apparent in other aspects of the colony's criminal law, that persistent criminal conduct, in the face of clear warning and exhortation, was more deserving of punishment than the single commission of a wrongful act. The remainder of the additions specify the kinds of utterances which are to be punished as blasphemous and are not greatly at variance with the common-law definition of blasphemy that appears in Blackstone at the end of the eighteenth century.

Curiously, the language of the colony's homicide provisions, which were enacted originally in 1641 and reenacted without change in the 1648 codification, contains few biblical terms. "Wilfull murder," "manslaughter," and "premeditated malice" were common-law terms, as were "mere casualty against will" and "mans necessary and just defence." The substance of at least one of these provisions, however, was not English but biblical. Homicide committed "suddenly in. . .ANGER, or CRUELTY of passion," was a mandatory capital crime pursuant to Numbers 35:20, whereas under English law homicide under such circumstances was manslaughter and a clergyable offense. Whether the murder statute, which appears on its face to make self-defense and lack of intention complete defenses, was based upon biblical authority is not entirely clear, but under English law homicide *se defendendo* and *per infortunium* were nevertheless crimes, although not felonies.

The colonial prescription of the death penalty for adultery reflected not only biblical influence but the Puritan view that the family was the cornerstone of church and commonwealth. Hence, any threat to the sanctity and integrity of the family unit deserved the most serious punishment of which God's law approved. Three generations of Puritan pamphleteers in England had advocated that adultery be punished by death instead of by the small fines and penances which the Archdeacon's Court normally imposed, and even Winthrop, for all his leniency in many directions, regarded as absurd the notion that "we may passe by Murders, Adulteryes, Idolatryes, etc: without Capitall punishments. . . ." Hence, the colonial law provided that "If any person committ ADULTERIE with a married, or espoused wife; the Adulterer & Adulteresse shal surely be put to death." Here, again, the Bible provided the substantive formulation of, and the penalty for, the crime. In accordance with Mosaic law, Massachusetts defined adultery in terms of the matrimonial status of the woman, ignoring that of the man; whereas under English ecclesiastical law adultery was committed whenever either participant in the illicit act was married. A second departure from the English definition of adultery was the extension of the crime to include intercourse with a woman espoused but not yet married. This extension was clearly based upon the prescription of Deuteronomy 22:23 and 24, cited as authority both in the Cotton draft of laws and in the Body of Liberties, to the effect, "If a damsel that is a virgin be betrothed unto an husband, and a man find her in the city, and lie with her; Then ye shall bring them both out unto the gate of that city, and ye shall stone them with stones that they die. . ."

The Massachusetts rape statute is the only one of the capital laws for which scriptural authority is not cited, and the reason for the omission appears to be that by the laws of Moses the offense was punishable not by death but by payment of damages and by an injuction to marry the victim. At common law, rape was defined as consensual or forcible copulation with a female under ten and nonconsensual intercourse with a female over ten; the offense was a felony and punishable by death. By the 1640's, the increase of sexual crime had become a source of grave concern to the Massachusetts authorities, and Winthrop had argued that "by the equity of the law against sodomy" intercourse with a child should be punished with death, "for it is against nature as well as sodomy. . . ." When the shocking case of John Humfry's daughters came to light and it was discovered that between the ages of seven and nine the elder had had sexual relations with three servants of her father, "so as she was grown capable of man's fellowship, and took pleasure in it," the colony was in an uproar. By English law, the men would have been hanged, and many in the General Court strongly urged the death penalty. Ultimately, after consultation with all the elders of Massachusetts, Plymouth, Connecticut, and New Haven, the court concluded that because the crime was not expressly capital by the word of God or by any express law of the colony the principal offender should be fined and have his nostrils slit and seared and should be required to wear a noose of rope around his neck. The other two men were also fined and ordered to be severely whipped. However, on the same day that sentence was passed, the General Court enacted its first addition to the capital laws of the Body of Liberties in the form of statutes prescribing mandatory death penalties for sexual intercourse, consensual or otherwise, with a child under ten and for forcible intercourse with a woman "married or contracted," and a discretionary death penalty for rape of any single woman above the age of ten.

These enactments afford striking illustrations of the interplay of cultural forces in the shaping of the colony law. The inference is clear that the General Court, shocked and inflamed by the Humfry case, formulated a definition of rape that bore a close similarity to the common-law crime but justified it on the basis of scriptural authority for the punishment of sodomy. From this standpoint, the subsequent history of the rape statutes is instructive. In the revision of the capital laws that preceded the codification of 1648, the two provisions imposing the mandatory death penalty were dropped from the capital laws, leaving only the law which related to forcible intercourse with a maid or single woman above the age of ten years and which decreed "death, or. . .some other greivous punishment according to circumstances as the Judges, or General court shal determin." It seems probable that the scruples about a "warrant" from the word of God that had saved the lives of the defendants in the Humfry case had sufficiently revived so that the General Court was unwilling to retain a mandatory death penalty which had no specific biblical authority.

The provisions of the Massachusetts capital laws have been discussed in some detail because they illustrate not only the colonists' extensive reliance upon Scripture but also their unwillingness to follow its precepts when contrary to their own ethical and moral conceptions. Despite their dependence upon the word of God and the close connection that they saw between sin and crime, they were demonstrably reluctant to prescribe death for every offense that the Bible ordered so punished. Had they regarded the Bible's pronouncements as dogmatic injunctions, literally to be followed under all circumstances, the criminal laws should have embraced at least as many capital offenses as John Cotton included in his draft code. In fact, the laws of Massachusetts prescribed relatively mild punishments for a number of such offenses, and the colonists' position seems to have been that no divine warrant was needed for the infliction of penalties that were *less* severe than those prescribed in the Bible. They were even more reluctant to extend the death penalty to offenses which were not expressly capital by the word of God, as the Humfry case illustrates. The General Court's decision in that case was entirely consistent with Puritan thinking on capital punishment. The author of the *Examen Legum Angliae*, who proposed reforms in the laws of England on the basis of biblical authority, stated it as "a Rule without Exception, given by the Learned, That no humane law can justly take away the life of a man for any offence, without a general or particular warrant from God's word; because mans life is onely at God's disposing."

In the criminal law, therefore, the authority of the Bible appears to have been sought less as a dogmatic rule to be blindly followed than as a justification, or "warrant" as the colonists termed it, for the infliction of death upon a fellow man. Within the limits for the reasons suggested, they apparently felt free to determine what offenses should be so punished. Hence, the scriptural annotations to the capital laws provided the justification, although not necessarily the reason, for their choice. In this connection it is worth observing that before 1650 there were but few convictions under any of the capital laws and, under some of them, none. This suggests that to a substantial extent, at least, those laws were believed, like the Decalogue, to fulfill a hortatory or *in terrorem* function, which is further emphasized by the order of the General Court that children be taught to read so that they would know the capital laws.

Among the reasons for the paucity of convictions under the capital laws was the insistence of the courts upon clear and palpable proof of the commission of crime. That insistence resulted partly from general Puritan reluctance to take human life and partly from the precept of Deuteronomy 17:6 that "At the mouth of two witnesses, or three witnesses, shall he that is worthy of death be put to death; but at the mouth of one witness he shall not be put to death." The colony law specifically prescribed that "no man shall be put to death without the testimonie of two or three *witnesses*, or that which is equivalent therunto." Although in the seventeenth century the two-witness rule was customarily followed in the English ecclesiastical courts in the Star Chamber, the common-law courts were moving away from the requirement of a fixed number of witnesses except in cases of treason and perjury. That tendency, together with the colonists' discussion and use of the rule, emphasizes its biblical basis. Not only were they sufficiently concerned about its scope to refer the problem to the elders of the churches, but they were prepared to, and apparently did, extend it, in accordance with the provision in John Cotton's draft code, to civil as well as criminal cases. Nevertheless, the adoption of the two-witness rule probably owed something to the colonists' English experience, and it is not without significance that Sir John Fortescue's fifteenth century treatise in praise of the laws of England referred to the law of God as forbidding proof by fewer than two witnesses.

The capital laws are by no means the only part of the colonial criminal law that reflect biblical influence. The limitation on whipping sentences to forty stripes, in contrast with the English formula "until his body be bloody," was apparently based upon Deuteronomy 25:2 and 3. Similarly, the fornication statute, which empowered the magistrates to enjoin the parties to marriage was clearly agreeable to the Word as set forth in Exodus 22:16, as contrasted with the then current practice of English justices of the peace, who were primarily concerned with the economic problem of fixing responsibility for support of a bastard child upon its reputed father. The Massachusetts law, however, had a further purpose in prescribing the marriage of the guilty parties, and that was the moral issue connected with the colonists' belief in the sanctity of the family unit and their conception of its role in community life. Here, again, in the adoption of the biblical rule, can be seen their insistence upon conforming their laws to the patterns of right living that had been developed in the colony.

Another striking departure from English law which apparently owed much to biblical authority was the colonists' adoption of multiple restitution and involuntary servitude for theft. At common law, the theft of a shilling, like other felonies, was punishable by hanging, and theft of a lesser amount by whipping. Under a number of English statutes, restitution—single, double, or treble—was a common penalty imposed by justices of the peace for a variety of specified property crimes. The Bible, however, prescribed multiple restitution as the penalty of the thief in most cases, or "if he have nothing, then he shall be sold for his theft."

From the beginning, the colonial magistrates regularly followed the biblical patterns, imposing double restitution when the offender was capable thereof, and requiring thieves unable to make restitution otherwise to satisfy the court's sentence by a term of service. The exaction of these penalties was without specific statutory authority until 1646. Prior thereto, the colonial treatment of theft furnishes an example of the shaping of law by magisterial discretion in the way favored by Winthrop. When restitution was feasible, it was usually the only punishment imposed, but the courts did not hesitate to combine it with one or more of a variety of other penalties, ranging through whipping, the stocks, a fine to the court, and degradation from the rank of gentleman. Servants, and others incapable of making restitution in money or in kind, were generally whipped, but theft by a servant from his own master appears to have been punished almost invariably by restitution, which was sometimes exacted in the form of an extension of the servant's term of service. Significantly, when the colonists enacted the theft act of 1646, they not only displaced the magistrates' discretionary power to vary penalties to which they had so long been opposed but adopted the English statutory penalty of treble restitution with which they had been familiar in rural England. Thus, while the early use of restitution as a penalty for theft can be attributed with reasonable assurance to biblical influence, its later statutory prescription is reflective of English ways. The colonial practice in this area again vividly illustrates the interplay of the two cultural forces.

The foregoing account of the role of the Bible in shaping the criminal law of the colony demonstrates that its influence was important but not always controlling. When we turn from the criminal to the civil law of the colony, however, the appar nt influence of the Bible is much less clear. Aside from the double portion allowed to the eldest son in cases of intestacy, and the prohibitions against bond slavery and usury, few provisions in the civil law can be attributed to scriptural influences. In one respect, however—namely, in the law of master and servant—those influences are unmistakable.

As already stated, a master was not only privileged, but under a duty, to correct his servant, and the servant might resort to the courts for protection against unjust or excessive correction. One of the provisions of the Body of Liberties, retained without substantial change in the Code of 1648, provided:

> If any servants shall flee from the Tiranny and crueltie of their masters to the howse of any freeman of the same Towne, they shall be there protected and susteyned till due order be taken for their relife. Provided due notice thereof be speedily given to their maisters from whom they fled. And the next Assistant or Constable where the partie flying is harboured.

The provision had a sound biblical precedent in Deuteronomy 23:15 and 16:

> Thou shalt not deliver unto his master the servant which is escaped from his master unto thee; He shall dwell with thee, even among you, in that place which he shall choose in one of thy gates, where it liketh him best: thou shalt not oppress him.

Characteristically, however, the Massachusetts law expanded the biblical rule by limiting the permissible grounds for self-help to "Tiranny and crueltie," and by ensuring the observance of due process of law through the requirement that proper notice be given to the servant's master and to an officer of the court. The effect of the colonial act was thus to give the oppressed servant an effective means of invoking the jurisdiction of the court to correct abuses, while also protecting the master's contractual rights.

A further provision of the colony laws which had explicit scriptural authority, decreed:

> If any man smite out the eye or tooth of his man-servant, or maid servant, or otherwise mayme or much disfigure him, unlesse it be by meere casualtie, he shall let them goe free from his service. And shall have such further recompense as the Court shall allow him.

A corresponding passage in Exodus 21:26-27 states that

> . . .if a man smite the eye of his servant, or the eye of his maid, that it perish; he shall let him go free for his eye's sake. And if he smite out his manservant's tooth, or his maidservant's tooth; he shall let him go free for his tooth's sake.

Again the colonists expanded the scriptural formula. Restating verbatim the eye-and-tooth provisions, the Massachusetts law nevertheless used them as the basis for framing a general rule that servants should be freed in any case of maiming or "much" disfigurement, and added the important qualification that the master's act must be deliberate.

Still another of the "Liberties of Servants" enacted in 1641 and incorporated into the Code declared:

> Servants that have served deligentlie and faithfully to the benefitt of their maisters seaven years, shall not be sent away emptie. And if any

have been unfaithfull, negligent or unprofitable in their service, notwithstanding the good usage of their maisters, they shall not be dismissed till they have made satisfaction according to the Judgement of Authoritie.

Deuteronomy 15:12-14, had said that servants were to be freed upon completion of seven years' service:

. . .in the seventh year thou shalt let him go free from thee. And when thou sendest him out free from thee, thou shalt not let him go away empty: Thou shalt furnish him liberally out of thy flock, and out of thy floor, and out of thy winepress: of that wherewith the Lord thy God hath blessed thee thou shalt give unto him.

Once more, and characteristically, the Massachusetts law incorporated inferences drawn from the bare text of Scripture. Only the good and faithful servant was entitled to a provision upon departing his master's service; more importantly, the negligent, unfaithful, or unprofitable servant was deemed obligated to make satisfaction for his shortcomings.

For all the biblical flavor of the colonial master-servant legislation, the Massachusetts courts' procedures for resolving disputes in this area did not greatly differ from contemporary English practices under the Statute of Labourers. In such cases, a single justice of the peace was empowered to "take such order and direction between the said master and his apprentice, as the equity of the cause shall require." Appeal was allowed by either party to the next sessions of the peace, where four justices were empowered to put an end to the indentures between master and apprentice, or "if the default shall be found to be in the apprentice, then the said justices. . .shall cause such due correction and punishment to be ministered unto him, as by their wisdom and discretions shall be thought meet." The Massachusetts rule, which permitted the mistreated servant to flee to the protection of a neighbor, who was thereupon obliged to notify the judicial authorities and the servant's master, had no statutory counterpart in England, but the disposition of such cases by the courts followed much the same pattern on both sides of the ocean. At Salem in 1645, Daniel Rumble, who confessed to striking Henry Hall in the head with a hand hammer, was fined and admonished for "Crueltie in Correcting" his servant. By comparison, in Worcestershire in 1637 a man was presented at the sessions of the peace "for immoderately beating and misusing Owen Brown his apprentice." In 1640 the Court of Assistants, finding that Samuel Hefford had "bene much misused by his master Jonathan Wade," freed him from Wade's service and put him out to another master for the remainder of his time. Similarly, an order of a Somerset quarter sessions in 1630 declared:

Whereas it hath appeared unto this Court that William Culverhouse of Greinton, Blacksmith, hath misued and beaten ffrancis Sheppard *als.* Townsend his apprentice to the great hurt of the said apprentice we doe therefore for preventinge of further mischeife which may happen absolutely free, acquit and discharge the said ffrancis Sheppard the apprentice from his apprenticehood. . . .

Thus, both the English and the Massachusetts systems enforced obedience, respect, and industry on the part of the servant, as well as rough standards of fair and humane treatment on the part of the master. The criteria applied in the colony undoubtedly owed as much to English precedent as to the Bible's texts. At the same time, the substantive similarity that each system bore to biblical precept suggests that Elizabethan legislators, like those of Massachusetts, were also influenced, though to a lesser degree, by the biblical inheritance in which they both shared.

BROOKS ADAMS (1848-1927), member of a family celebrated in American history, was a younger brother of the historian Henry Adams. Brooks and another brother, Charles Francis, Jr., wrote extensively on the early history of Massachusetts, their native state. Though historians by avocation, the Adamses consciously adopted the standards of "scientific" history then being produced by the first professional historians in America. Brooks's approach to Puritanism was also influenced by his family background. Inheriting a traditional antipathy to the "Brahmin" social class that reigned over Boston, he took delight in denouncing the unscientific "filiopietism" of Brahmin historians who deliberately overlooked or tried to excuse the lapses of their Puritan ancestors. In contrast to the filiopietists' praise, Brooks, in *The Emancipation of Massachusetts,* attacks the Puritans for their bigotry and intolerance, which he blames largely upon the ministers.°

The Rule of the Priesthood

The seventeenth century was aristocratic, and the inhabitants of the larger part of New England were divided into three classes, the commonalty, the gentry, and the clergy. Little need be said of the first, except that they were a brave and determined race, as ready to fight as Cromwell's saints, who made Rupert's troopers "as stubble to their swords;" that they were intelligent, and would not brook injustice; and that they were resolute, and would not endure oppression. All know that they were energetic and shrewd.

The gentry had the weight in the community that comes with wealth and education, and they received the deference then paid to birth, for they were for the most part the descendants of English country-gentlemen. As a matter of course they monopolized the chief offices; and they were not sentenced by the courts to degrading punishments, like whipping, for their offences, as other criminals were. . . .

Yet notwithstanding the existence of this aristocratic element, the real substance of influence and power lay with the clergy. It has been taught as an axiom of Massachusetts history, that from the outset the town was the social and political unit; but an analysis of the evidence tends to show that the organization of the Puritan Commonwealth was ecclesiastical, and the congregation, not the town, the basis upon which the fabric rested. By the consti-

°Reprinted from Brooks Adams, *The Emancipation of Massachusetts* (Boston: Houghton Mifflin Company, 1921), pp. 195-206. Footnotes omitted.

tution of the corporation the franchise went with the freedom of the company; but in order to form a constituency which would support a sacerdotal oligarchy, it was enacted in 1631 "that for time to come noe man shalbe admitted to the freedome of this body polliticke, but such as are members of some of the churches within. . .the same." Thus though communicants were not necessarily voters, no one could be a voter who was not a communicant; therefore the town-meeting was in fact nothing but the church meeting, possibly somewhat attenuated, and called by a different name. By this insidious statute the clergy seized the temporal power, which they held till the charter fell. The minister stood at the head of the congregation and moulded it to suit his purposes and to do his will; for though he could not when opposed admit an inhabitant to the sacrament, he could peremptorily exclude therefrom all those of whom he disapproved, for "none are propounded to the congregation, except they be first allowed by the elders." In such a community the influence of the priesthood must have been overwhelming. . . .

Nor was their power bounded by local limits; though seldom holding office themselves, they were solemnly consulted by the government on every important question that arose, whether of war or peace, and their counsel was rarely disregarded. They gave their opinion, no matter how foreign the subject might be to their profession or their education; and they had no hesitation in passing upon the technical construction of the charter with the authority of a bench of judges. An amusing example is given by Winthrop: "The General Court assembled again, and all the elders were sent for, to reconcile the differences between the magistrates and deputies. When they were come the first question put to them was, . . .whether the magistrates are, by patent and election of the people, the standing council of this commonwealth in the vacancy of the General Court, and have power accordingly to act in all cases subject to government, according to the said patent and the laws of this jurisdiction; and when any necessary occasions call for action from authority, in cases where there is no particular express law provided, there to be guided by the word of God, till the General Court give particular rules in such cases. The elders, having received the question, withdrew themselves for consultation about it, and the next day sent to know, when we would appoint a time that they might attend the court with their answer. The magistrates and deputies agreed upon an hour" and. . ."their answer was affirmative, on the magistrates behalf, in the very words of the question, with some reasons thereof. It was delivered in writing by Mr. Cotton in the name of them all, they being all present, and not one dissentient."

Then the magistrates propounded four more questions, the last of which is as follows: "Whether a judge be bound to pronounce such sentence as a positive law prescribes, in case it be apparently above or beneath the merit of the offence?" To which the elders replied at great length, saying that the penalty must vary with the gravity of the crime, and added examples: "So any sin committed with an high hand, as the gathering of sticks on the Sabbath day, may be punished with death when a lesser punishment may serve for gathering sticks privily and in some need." Yet though the clerical influence was so unbounded the theocracy itself was exposed to constant peril. In monarchies such as France or Spain the priests who rule the king have the force of the nation at command to dispose of at their will; but in Massachusetts a more difficult problem was presented, for the voters had to be controlled. By the law requiring freemen to be church-members the elders meant to grasp the key to the suffrage, but experience soon proved that more stringent regulation was needed.

According to the original Congregational theory each church was complete and independent, and elected its own officers and conducted its own worship, free from interference from without, except that others of the same communion might offer advice or admonition. Under the theocracy no such loose system was possible, for heresy might enter in three different ways; first, under the early law, "blasphemers" might form a congregation and from thence creep into the company; second, an established church might fall into error; third, an unsound minister might be chosen, who would debauch his flock by securing the admission of sectaries to the sacrament. Above all, a creed was necessary by means of which false doctrine might be instantly detected and condemned. Accordingly, one by one, as the need for vigilance increased, laws were passed to guard these points of danger.

First, in 1635 it was enacted, "Forasmuch as it hath bene found by sad experience, that much trouble and disturbance hath happened both to the church & civill state by the officers & members of some churches, which have bene gathered. . .in an undue manner. . .it is. . .ordered that. . .this Court doeth not, nor will hereafter, approue of any such companyes of men as shall henceforthe ioyne in any pretended way of church fellowshipp, without they shall first acquainte the magistrates, & the elders of the great pte of the churches in this jurisdicon, with their intencons, and have their approbacon herein. And ffurther, it is ordered, that noe pson, being a member of any churche which shall hereafter be gathered without the approbacon of the magistrates, & the greater pte of the said churches, shallbe admitted to the ffreedome of this comonwealthe."

In 1648 all the elders met in a synod at Cambridge; they adopted the Westminster Confession of Faith and an elaborate "Platform of Church Discipline," the last clause of which is as follows: "If any church. . .shall grow schismatical, rending itself from the communion of other churches, or shall walk incorrigibly and obstinately in any corrupt way of their own contrary to the rule of the word; in such case the magistrate, . . .is to put forth his coercive power, as the matter shall require."

In 1658 the General Court declared: "Whereas it is the duty of the Christian magistrate to take care the people be fed wth wholesome & sound doctrine, & in this houre of temptation, . . .it is therefore ordered, that henceforth no person shall. . .preach to any company of people, whither in church society or not, or be ordeyned to the office of a teaching elder, where any two organnick churches, councill of state, or Generall Court shall declare theire dissatisfaction thereat, either in refference to doctrine or practize. . .and in case of ordination. . .timely notice thereof shall be given unto three or fower of the neighbouring organicke churches for theire approbation." And lastly, in 1679, the building of meeting-houses was forbidden, without leave from the freemen of the town or the General Court.

But legislation has never yet controlled the action of human thought. All experience shows that every age, and every western nation, produces men whose nature it is to follow the guidance of their reason in the face of every danger. To exterminate these is the task of religious persecution, for they can be silenced only by death. Thus is a dominant priesthood brought face to face with the alternative of surrendering its power or of killing the heretic, and those bloody deeds that cast their sombre shadow across the history of the Puritan Commonwealth cannot be seen in their true bearing unless the position of the clergy is vividly before the mind.

Cromwell said that ministers were "helpers of, not lords over, God's people," but the orthodox New Englander was the vassal of his priest. Winthrop was the ablest and the most enlightened magistrate the ecclesiastical party ever had, and he tells us that "I honoured a faithful minister in my heart and could have kissed his feet." If the governor of Massachusetts and the leader of the emigration could thus describe his moral growth,—a man of birth, education, and fortune, who had had wide experience of life, and was a lawyer by profession,—the awe and terror felt by the mass of the communicants can be imagined.

Jonathan Mitchel, one of the most famous of the earlier divines, thus describes his flock: "They were a gracious, savoury-spirited people, principled by Mr. Shepard, liking an humbling, mourning, heart-breaking ministry and spirit; living in religion, praying men and women." And "he would speak with such a transcendent majesty and liveliness, that the people. . .would often shake under his dispensations, as if they had heard the sound of the trumpets from the burning mountain, and yet they would mourn to think, that they were going presently to be dismissed from such an heaven upon earth.". . ."When a publick admonition was to be dispensed unto any one that had offended scandalously. . .the hearers would be all drowned in tears, as if the admonition had been, as indeed he would with much artifice make it be directed unto them all; but such would be the compassion, and yet the gravity, the majesty, the scriptural and awful pungency of these his dispensations, that the conscience of the offender himself, could make no resistance thereunto."

Their arrogance was fed by the submission of the people, and they would not tolerate the slightest opposition even from their most devoted retainers. The Reforming Synod was held in 1679. "When the report of a committee on 'the evils that had provoked the Lord' came up for consideration, 'Mr. Wheelock declared that there was a cry of injustice in that magistrates and ministers were not rated' (taxed), 'which occasioned a very warm discourse. Mr. Stodder' (minister of Northampton) 'charged the deputy with saying what was not true, and the deputy governor' (Danforth) 'told him he deserved to be laid by the heels, etc.'

" 'After we broke up, the deputy and several others went home with Mr. Stodder, and the deputy asked forgiveness of him and told him he freely forgave him, but Mr. Stodder was high.' The next day 'the deputy owned his being in too great a heat, and desired the Lord to forgive it, and Mr. Stodder did something, though very little, by the deputy.' " Wheelock was lucky in not having to smart more severely for his temerity, for the unfortunate Ursula Cole was sentenced to pay £5 or be whipped for the lighter crime of saying "she had as lief hear a cat mew" as Mr. Shepard preach. . . .

Common men could not have kept this hold upon the inhabitants of New England, but the clergy were learned, resolute, and able, and their strong but narrow minds burned with fanaticism and love of power; with their beliefs and under their temptations persecution seemed to them not only their most potent weapon, but a duty they owed to Christ—and that duty they unflinchingly performed. John Cotton, the most gifted among them, taught it as a holy work: "But the good that is brought to princes and subjects by the due punishment of apostate seducers and idolaters and blasphemers is manifold.

"First, it putteth away evill from the people and cutteth off a gangreene, which would spread to further ungodlinesse. . . .

"Secondly, it driveth away wolves from worrying and scattering the sheep of Christ. For false teachers be wolves, . . .and the very name of wolves holdeth forth what benefit will redound to the sheep, by either killing them or driving them away.

"Thirdly, such executions upon such evill doers causeth all the country to heare and feare, and doe no more such wickednesse. . . . Yea as these punishments are preventions of like wickednesse in some, so are they wholesome medicines, to heale such as are curable of these eviles. . . .

"Fourthly, the punishments executed upon false prophets and seducing teachers, doe bring downe showers of God's blessings upon the civill state. . . .

"Fifthly, it is an honour to God's Justice that such judgments are executed. . . ."

All motives combined to drive them headlong into cruelty; for in the breasts of the larger number, even the passion of bigotry was cool beside the malignant hate they felt for those whose opinions menaced their earthly power and dominion; and they never wearied of exhorting the magistrates to destroy the enemies of the church.

In the middle 1940s, when the revisionist case was gradually gaining ground, AARON B. SEIDMAN reconsidered one of the major premises of the theocratic historians, that the ministers controlled the machinery of government in the early years of the Holy Commonwealth. Seidman traces the relationship between the ministers and the political leaders as it was defined in formal law and as it functioned in political and religious affairs. In each instance he finds the magistrates effectively dominating the ministers instead of the other way around. Within the context of his argument, he reappraises such events as the law of 1631, which limited freemanship to church members, and concludes that the civil magistrates had their own reasons for favoring this measure.°

Church and State Reconsidered

Discussions of the relationship between the clerical and civil polities that existed in early Massachusetts have tended to foster concepts of inextricability. What is more, the Puritan clergy is usually accredited with the power of swaying governmental decisions to a highly impressive extent. Especially does this hold true for the period immediately following the founding of the Massachusetts Bay Colony: 1630-1660. This paper will attempt to evaluate the relative position of church and state during these three decades.

In the main, investigations of the status of the church have as their premise the extensive influence of that body in secular affairs. Accepting this postulate, many scholars and historians have assumed the complete identification of civil and ecclesiastical functions in the Puritan Commonwealth. This emphasis on extreme clerical power and the uncritical use of such terms as *theocracy* and *Biblical Commonwealth* have obscured, to a degree, some pertinent facts of early Massachusetts history. . . .

The beginnings of the colony point clearly to the shrewdness, foresight, and tenacity of its secular leaders. These qualities are reflected in the clear-headed

---

°From A. B. Seidman, "Church and State in the Early Years of the Massachusetts Bay Colony," *New England Quarterly*, XVIII (1945), pp. 211-233. Reprinted with the footnotes omitted by permission of the managing editor of The New England Quarterly

manner in which they outlined their aims for Massachusetts. Both they and the clergy realized that the religious were not the sole considerations prompting the migration. The leaders themselves did not neglect the material reasons for voyaging to New England. These reasons motivated their desire for a strong civil government, at times even to the exclusion and detriment of the church. The strength of the secular governmental leaders and their masterful tactics of entrenching their power continue to be evident throughout the organization of the New England Colony. Most marked as a means of fortifying civil power was an insistence upon the classification of civil and ecclesiastical functions as separate entities.

Evidence of this separation is contained in Winthrop's *A Modell of Christian Charity.* While the Puritans were still on the ship which was bringing them to American in 1630, Governor Winthrop wrote this essay setting forth the underlying principles which he believed the infant government should follow. He stressed, for the benefit of this group of hardy settlers, that they set sail ". . .to seeke out a place of Cohabitation and Consorteshipp under a due form of Government both *civill and ecclesiasticall. . . .*"

John Winthrop's distinction between the civil and ecclesiastical aspects of the government was clearly expounded by the Reverend John Cotton to the Lord Say and Seal, in 1636. Sketching his views of church and state, Cotton writes:

> When your lordship doubteth, that this corse will draw all things under the determination of the church, . . .(seeing that the church is to determine who shall be members, and none but a member may hav to doe in the government of a commonwealth) be pleased (I pray you) to conceyve, that *magistrates are neyther chosen to office in the church, nor doe governe by directions from the church, but by civill lawes,* . . .

Further substantiation of the sundering of civil and church affairs can be found in Winthrop's speech, in 1637, at the conclusion of the Antinomian crisis. In his *Journal,* Winthrop writes that many members of the Boston church were angered at the governor for his proceedings in the crisis. They did not press the issue, but he ". . .thought fit to prevent such a public disorder, and so took occasion to speak to the congregation to this effect: 1. That if he had been called, etc., he would have desired first, to have advised with the elders, *whether the church had power to call in question the proceedings of the civil court.*"

With the formation of the Body of Liberties, in 1641, these expressions of the division between church and state and of the ascendancy of civil authority were consolidated into a form of standing law for the commonwealth. Law 58 states that "Civill Authoritie hath power and libertie to see the peace, ordinances and Rules of Christ observed in every church according to his word, so it be done in a *Civill and not in an Ecclesiastical way.*" Law 95, section 8, limits ecclesiastical authority by decreeing: "All Churches have libertie to deale with any of their members in a church way that are in the hand of Justice. So it be not to retard or hinder the course thereof." The church had no power to "retard or hinder" the course of civil authority. And should the phrases *to deale with* or *in a church way* seem to give the church leeway by virtue of their vagueness, the court reserved for itself the power of deciding doubtful cases and matters that required interpretation: ". . .and whensoever there shall arise any question in any Court amonge the Assistants and Associates thereof about the explanation of these Rites and liberties, the Generall Court onely shall have the power to interprett them." Furthermore doubly to insure the absence of clerical interference, laws 59 and 60 announce boldly: "Civill Authoritie hath power and libertie to deale with any Church member in a way of Civill Justice, notwithstanding any Church relation, office or interest." "No church censure shall degrade or depose any man from any Civill dignitie, office, or Authoritie he shall have in the Commonwealth." It is abundantly clear that the intention of these laws was sharply to define the limits of church and state, thus preventing the church from overreaching its prerogatives.

It is easier to appreciate the Puritan's desire to keep clear the demarcation between church and state affairs when we consider the country of their origin. The Puritans had travelled from England for an unknown land to establish new homes. They still smarted under the persecutions of the Church of England, and the harryings of this hierarchy were fresh in their minds. They therefore feared to implant in their midst another clergy with such undue influence that it might eventually grasp the reins of government. This resolution was given weight by the incident of the archbishops. It must have been a fear-kindling experience for the men of that day when they learned of the event which Governor John Winthrop recorded in his *Journal* for September 18, 1634:

> . . .there came over a copy of the commission granted to the two archbishops and ten others of the council, to regulate all plantations, and power given them, or any five of them, to call in all patents, to make laws, to raise tythes and portions for ministers, *to remove and punish governors,* and to hear and determine all causes, and inflict all punishments, even death itself,. . .

This commission which was intended to replace the Puritan government never crossed the Atlantic. Small wonder, however, that in these sweeping rights granted the prospective archbishops, the Puritans should have discerned a source of great peril, one, which in all probability intensified their dislike of a hierarchy.

All this evidence leads to one conclusion: in spirit, in theory, and in practice, Massachusetts was not a church-dominated state, and that, from the start, incipient seeds of the later complete division between church and state were already active. . . .

The march of the secular leaders toward firmly entrenched power is illustrated by the question of suffrage in which the magistrates definitely employed the church as a limiting agent. The right to vote was already confined to freemen, and the civil leaders soon carried this selective process a step further. The right to become a freeman, they ruled, could be awarded only to those who were church members. Many scholars have cited this fact as evidence of church surveillance over state affairs. This assumption, however, is incorrect. The limitation of suffrage was simply a matter of expediency. If the government were to be thrown open to everyone, the existent magistrates would have lost every vestige of control, and they were well aware of the fact.

With the use of church membership as a bar, the magistrates effectively protected themselves. The following restriction of suffrage was entered in the Company Records on May 18, 1631:

> . . .& to the end the body of comons may be pserued [preserved] by honest & good men, it was likewise ordered and agreed that for time to come noe man shalbe admitted to the freedome of this body polliticke, but such as are members of some of the churches within the lymitts of the same.

In view of the tenacious grasp of the civil rulers on the government, this law cannot be interpreted as an encroachment of the church on civil affairs, but rather as evidence of the means used by the secular leaders in retaining their mastery. . . .

For these purposes the clergy proved useful, and thus found entrance into legislative circles. They were summoned to aid the civil officials who were jealous of their sovereignty and wary even of the church. When the deputies questioned the arbitrary power assumed by the magistrates, and the magistrates claimed this power as their right, the ministers were consulted.

In 1634, the magistrates were confronted with the case of the "negative voice," in which the Reverend John Cotton saved the day for them. The assistants claimed that the charter delegated to them "the negative voice," or veto power. The deputies bitterly contested this power demanded by the assistants. After a deadlock had been reached, Dr. Cotton preached a sermon, favoring the acceptance of "a negative voice" for the magistrates. After the sermon Winthrop noted that ". . .it pleased the Lord so as to assist him, . . .that the affairs of the court went on cheerfully. . ." Thus the assistants received their "negative voice." The clergy had served to turn the balance of a contested issue in favor of the elder magistrates.

The magisterial powers adopted by the rulers were not incontestably written in the charter. Instead the jurisdictional functions assumed by the civil government had to be inferred from the language of the original document. In 1644 when the magistrates and the deputies were at odds over this issue, the church favored the magistrates. The question of the deputies was: ". . .Whether the titles of governor, deputy, and assistants do necessarily imply magistratical authority, in the patent? The elders' answer was affirmative."

Thus when the clergy were called in, it was to assist the court generally or to advise in cases where disputes arose that had to be settled in favor of the magistrates. Yet it was always distinctly understood that church and state were to be kept as separate agencies. Keeping this fact in mind, we can understand the meaning of a pronouncement by Governor Winthrop. On one occasion, he said that no member of the court should be questioned by a church for any speech made in a session of the court, because it ". . .may not fit to acquaint the church with, being a secret of state. . . ."

In another instance Winthrop reprimanded the elders for interfering in a dispute concerning the deputies and the magistrates, when they were not needed: "And some of the elders had done no good offices in this matter, through their misapprehensions both of the intentions of the magistrates and also of the matters themselves, being affairs of state, which did not belong to their calling." It is quite evident then that the magistracy employed the clergy and kept them distinct from the state. It will further be seen that when the clergy were summoned to the General Court, their function was confined to that of an advisory capacity. . . .

Furthermore, even before the migration, the Company decided that ministers were to retain a strictly advisory position when they were requested to appear before the court. As early as October 19, 1629, the court announced: ". . .if any difference happen which they [the court] cannot agree on, that then the same bee referred to the *umperage* & determinacon of some of the preachers. . .who are desired to sett downe in wryting what they shall thinke in conscience is fitt to bee done, . . ."[1] But nowhere is it stipulated that the umpire's advice must be accepted as final.

The magistrates' power, derived from the charter, was of an inclusive nature. They retained it, in part, by confining the

[1] Italics the author's.

privileges of freemen to favored church members. When the freemen became restive and their delegates forced concessions to demands for popular government, the General Court took unto itself the selection of the freemen. The deputies, however, remained a constant thorn in the side of the magistrates. Against this and the threat of other popular incursions, the secular leaders sought aid and they found it in the judicious use of the church and the clergy.

The government of the Bay Colony has often been held up as the classic example of church and state operating as one unit. In effect, however, the character and degree of church participation in governmental affairs was limited to a number of fairly well defined functions. We have already noted some cases in which the church was employed by the magistrates to strengthen their political position. A series of other instances will serve to illustrate a further limitation of extent to which the church has been said to have participated in civil affairs. We shall see that when clergymen were summoned to the General Court, they were asked to resolve impasses between high officials; they unravelled issues involving the moral implications, and preached sermons of a general character before the election of the governor and the assistants. At all events, their advice was voted upon, but it was not necessarily accepted.

In practice it will be seen that the ministers were consulted when conflicts between governing personalities arose—quite often those of Winthrop and Dudley. In his *Journal*, John Winthrop quotes such a case in which the Reverend Mr. Wilson and the Reverend Mr. Welde were called to the court on August 3, 1632. After the meeting of arbitration, Winthrop dutifully recorded ". . .himself faulty. . . ."

Minister John Cotton concerned himself with a civil problem wherein he discerned a moral implication. In 1641, Winthrop writes:

> At this session, Mr. Hathorn, one of the deputies, and usually one of their speakers, made a motion to some other of the deputies of leaving out two of their ancientest magistrates because they were grown poor, . . .

The Reverend John Cotton on hearing this, took occasion the next lecture day to reprove the resolution and its author. The justice of this admonition was felt, and Winthrop remarks that "This public reproof gave such a check to the former motion as it was never revived after. . . ." The Reverend Mr. Cotton had strong moral grounds for his support of the magistrates grown poor in the service of their country.

The participation of the church in civil affairs is further illustrated in the sermons which were preached before the election of a new governor and assistants. These sermons, in the main, did not partake of the nature ascribed to our modern campaign speeches. At best the clergyman delivering the sermon made only veiled allusions to certain favorable candidates. More often this kind of sermon commented on the general qualifications of good leaders without specific reference to any one person. The Reverend Thomas Shepard in an election sermon preached in 1638, warned the people not to choose "brambles" (*Judges* 9: 14, 15) for officials, as they would become misleaders. Again in 1669 the Reverend John Davenport, in an election sermon, remarked, "You must submit to their Authority, and perform all duties to them, whom you have chosen to be your Rulers,. . ."

Another election sermon preached in 1634 by the Reverend Mr. Ezekiel Rogers, pastor of the church in Rowley, is noted in Winthrop's *Journal.* Although the clergyman preaching the court election sermon was usually chosen by the magistrates, the Reverend Mr. Rogers was selected by the deputies. It is clear that they wanted to replace Winthrop as governor and, in all likelihood, they knew that Reverend Ezekiel Rogers would express his dislike of having a governor serve for two terms in succession. The Reverend Mr. Rogers was permitted to preach, and Winthrop writes that Mr. Rogers ". . .dissuaded them earnestly from choosing the same man twice together, and expressed his dislike of that with such vehemency as gave offence." The advice of Mr. Rogers was not taken, and Winthrop continues restrainedly:

. . .But when it came to trial, the former governor, Mr. Winthrop, was chosen again. . . .

Those scholars who insist upon emphasizing the power of the church in the secular affairs of the colony sometimes point to the fact that the *Body of Liberties*, accepted by the court as the law of the land, was compiled by a member of the clergy—the Reverend Nathaniel Ward. It must be kept in mind, however, that in 1636 John Cotton was asked to prepare a body of laws for the court. Winthrop notes that Mr. Cotton did present a model of "Moses His Judicials" to the court. Despite the Reverend Mr. Cotton's alleged power in secular affairs, his code was eventually rejected, and Mr. Ward's became the law of the Commonwealth. Moreover it was not Mr. Ward's preëminence as a clergyman which was responsible for the acceptance of his code. By 1641 when the *Body of Liberties* became legalized, Nathaniel Ward had ceased to serve as a minister in the colony. The reason for the acceptance of his code lay rather in the fact that he had been trained as a lawyer before coming to New England as a clergyman. Winthrop notes that Ward was ". . .formerly a student and practiser in the course of common law. . . ."

When considering the question of church participation in civil affairs, it is well to keep in mind a number of implied restraints which effectively served the General Court in its relations with the church. The first of these restraints, the fear of a hierarchy in the church, also existed among the ministers. For example, it had become a custom for the ministers of the Bay to meet once a fortnight at one of their homes where some question of moment was usually discussed. Complaints soon filtered in: "Mr. Skelton, the pastor of Salem, and Mr. Williams. . .took some exception against it, as fearing it might grow in time to a presbytery or superintendency, to the prejudice of the churchs' liberties." The fear of a church hierarchy and of church encroachment on civil authority was a real one, and its beginnings were combatted by churchmen and layleaders alike.

The second restraint lay in the fact that the ministers were literally exiles for nonconfirmity. In his *Memoirs* the Reverend Thomas Shepard tells how, in England, he had been forbidden to preach and could find no subsistence as a consequence. He and other clergymen in his position, however, found tolerable peace in New England, and it is difficult to believe that they would have endangered this security by antagonizing the civil leaders.

As to the third restraint, which concerned the livelihood of the ministers, it can be seen that no sooner had the first court of assistants convened in Charlestown, New England, in August, 1630, than there was an order issued for the financial support of the Reverend Mr. Wilson and the Reverend Mr. Phillips. In November of the same year another order described how the money was to be collected. And the court sought to enforce these provisions. When on October 23, 1657, it was reported that several of the ministers were not well provided for, that court ordered speediest arrangements made for their relief.

Thus, no matter what rôle the clergy played in civil questions, be it advisory, mediatory, or admonitory, the barriers between church and state were zealously maintained. The charter specified that the ministers were to be hired by the company and the company ruled that clergymen were to be called to the court only as umpires. Their advice, however, was not mandatory, and was not always accepted. The tacit restraints on the clergy, further fortified the position of the magistrates. Throughout the early life of the Colony, church participation in secular affairs was supervised and stringently limited.

Before ascribing to the clergy an inordinately large share of sway in matters secular, it is well to consider the position of the court in clerical matters. Did the church receive proscriptions or directions from the magistrates, and were the affairs of the church circumscribed by civil scrutiny? Furthermore, it would be significant if the ministers required aid from the court in the disciplining of their own parishioners.

The strong grasp of the governor and the assistants on the ecclesiastical life of the colony is amply documented in the colony records. The magistrates found it necessary to regulate the formation of churches, to approve the appointment of ministers, and to suppress offending ministers.

On March 3, 1635, it is recorded that because there had been several disturbances in certain churches newly formed in the colony, the court was compelled to take steps. After this time no churches were to be organized unless "...they shall first acquainte the magistrates...& have their approbacon herein..." Not only did the organization of all new churches need the approval of the court, but the choice of ministers was contingent on the magistrates. On May 19, 1658, the record stipulates that no preacher shall continue at his calling "...where any two organnick churches, councill of state, or *General Court* shall declare theire dissatisfaction thereat..."[2] Even as late as 1660 the court attempted to control the ministry. The County Courts are admonished concerning "...the purging of their tounes & peculiars from such ministry & publicke preachers as shallbe found vitious in theire liues and pernitiously hethrodoxe in theire doctrines, ..."

The breadth of civil power in church affairs can further be gauged by the court's summoning of synods. In 1646 some clergymen were incensed because they "...were not satisfied of any such power [to call synods] given by Christ to the civil magistrates over the churches in such cases..." It was finally agreed, however, that "...the civil magistrate had power upon *just occasion* to require the churches to send their messengers to advise in such ecclesiastical matters either of doctrine or discipline...,"[3] so that the "purity and truth" of the church might be protected. Clearly, then, the power of the court to interfere in church matters was restricted only by the magistrates' interpretation of what constituted a "just occasion." Note, inaddition, this statement as to the limited extent of the synod's power: "...the end of the synod was not to proceed by way of power, but only of counsel from the word of God, and *the court was at liberty either*

[2] Italics the author's.
[3] Italics the author's.

to establish or disannul such agreement of the synod, as they should see cause,. . ."[4] Thus, the power of civil leaders extended to affairs of the church proper, and they liberally interpreted their duties as protectors of the church and civil polities.

The provisions of the *Cambridge Platform*, completed by the Synod of 1648, are themselves indicative of the division of church and state and the extensive power of the civil government in affairs of the church. In chapter XVII, "Of the Civil Magistrates powr in Matters Ecclesiastical," it is written that: "As it is unlawfull for church-officers to meddle with the sword of the Magistrate, so it is unlawfull for the Magistrate to meddle with the work proper to church officers. . . ." Although this provision seems to exclude the civil government from participation in church affairs, such was not the case, as may readily be seen by noting the following requirements:

> It is the duty of the Magistrate, to take care of matters of religion, . . .The end of the Magistrates office, is not only the quiet & peaceful life of the subject, in matters of righteousness & honesty, but also in matters of godliness, yea of all godliness. . . .

Viewing these two ideas, the one ostensibly excluding the magistrate from "the work proper to church officers" and the other exhorting him "to take care of matters of religion," only one conclusion is possible. The magistrate, in order to maintain "godliness," was compelled to interfere in internal matters of the church. The church, furthermore, was told that it was "unlawfull for church-officers to meddle with the sword of the magistrate."

The government, furthermore, served as an arm of the church in punishing misdemeanors of a religious nature. The magistrates censured religious transgressions, and the lack of regular attendance at church on the Lord's Day; they proclaimed fasts and thanksgivings; discovered misdeeds and punished the wrong-doers. They served the church and so strengthened their own authority. They repeatedly interfered in what should have been church questions exclusively.

When there was a call to proclaim a day of thanksgiving it became a court order. When a complaint was entered, in 1634, against those people who absented themselves from meetings on the Lord's Day the court acted. To prevent this laxness, ". . .power. . .[was]. . .giuen to any two Assistants to heare & sensure, either by ffyne or imprisonmt. . .all misdemeanrs of that kinde. . . ." Cases of severe discipline for religious faults and heterodox opinion can be found in the court orders:

> It is ordered, that John Baker shalbe whipped for shooteing att fowle on the Sabboth day, etc.
>
> It is ordered that, Phillip Ratliffe shalbe whipped, haue his eares cutt off, fyned. . ., & banished. . .for vttering mallitious & scandulous speeches against the goumt & church of Salem, . . .

When members of the clergy made public speeches or committed acts which were considered wayward by the General Court, they were rapidly called to account. The court, at times, selected other churchmen to deal with the offenders. The [Roger] Williams case illustrates the civil censure of a clergyman. Another example is that of the teacher of the Church of Roxbury, the Reverend Mr. Eliot. Winthrop writes that Mr. Eliot had found fault with a proceeding of the court. "We took order, that he should be dealt with by Mr. Cotton, Mr. Hooker, and Mr. Welde, to be brought to see his errour, . . ." The Reverend Mr. Eliot was convinced and prom-

[4] Winthrop, *History of New England*, II, 323 (italics the author's).

ised to make a public apology the next Lord's Day.

Throughout, the secular government intruded upon numerous internal affairs of the church, both as far as ministers and parishioners were concerned. The conventional assertion that in the Massachusetts Bay Colony the church dominated the state, is not borne out by the facts; the reverse was true: the state dominated the church.

In the final analysis, we must note that to regard the early Massachusetts Bay Colony as a state completely influenced by the clergy is to ignore some striking facts. The government of the Bay Colony cannot be described as a veritable church-state in the sense that the civil, as well as the ecclesiastical power lay in the hands of the clergy In the documents of the colony and in the writings of its leading men, separation was constantly implied and expressed. At no time do we find church and state operating as one unit. Furthermore, secular power, based on the charter, rested firmly in the hands of the governor and the assistants, and religious affairs were, generally, subservient to policies of state. The magistrates employed the ministers to maintain their power, but the ministers came before the court as carefully guarded arbitrators. On the other hand, civil leaders dealt with affairs of a religious nature to an impressive extent. In fine, despite a certain amount of interaction between church and state in the Puritan Commonwealth of early Massachusetts, the essential boundaries of the two organizations were kept well defined, and any encroachment or predominating influence must be ascribed not to the church, but to the state.

The economic ideas of the Puritans in the seventeenth century are commonly referred to under the rubric of "the Protestant Ethic," a term first applied to them by the German sociologist Max Weber. This ethic—essentially an ethic of restraint—was taught in New England, where it was also used as the standard for judging economic behavior in specific instances. In this selection, part of a larger study, *The New England Merchants in the Seventeenth Century*, BERNARD BAILYN (1922- Winthrop Professor of American history at Harvard, describes the censure of a Boston merchant accused of violating the principle of a "just price." Bailyn is primarily interested in the conflict between the merchants' economic values and the values contained within the Protestant Ethic.°

The Merchants and the Protestant Ethic

Into the commercial situation of New England in 1630 the great Puritan Migration brought the first of the permanent merchants. Though clearly distinguishable from the interlopers, servants of English merchants, and Pilgrims who had preceded them in trade, they were not men of uniform background or training. Some whose origins lay in the lower levels of London's commercial populace were experienced tradesmen who put their skills to good use in the New World. Others, gentlemen and yeomen of rural England, found in the New World inducements to enter business for the first time.

Despite such differences all of the first generation Puritan merchants agreed that religious considerations were highly relevant to the conduct of trade, that commerce, being one of the many forms of human intercourse, required control by moral laws. But some of the newly arrived merchants, as they assumed power over the exchange of goods, felt the restrictive effect of these ideas when acted upon by a determined ministry and magistracy. In their confused reaction to ethical control as well as in the progress of their business enterprises lay seeds of social change. . . .

The ethical keystone of the great edifice of Calvinism was the conviction that all men were totally responsible for their be-

°Reprinted by permission of the publishers from Bernard Bailyn, *The New England Merchants in the Seventeenth Century* (Cambridge, Mass.: Harvard University Press), pp. 19-44. Copyright, 1955, by the President and Fellows of Harvard College. Footnotes omitted.

havior. The heart of the question, as a sixteenth-century writer put it, is not the quantity of sin but the fact that God's majesty is offended at all; "...be the thing never so little, yet the breach of his Commandment deserveth death."

To men for whom life was moral experience, no actions were more relevant to the overwhelming consideration of salvation than those touching the welfare of one's fellow men. For, however discouraging to those who found a righteous life a simpler matter when lived in solitude, the Puritan's obligation to live intensively as a social being was nothing less than God's will. Society was an organism functioning for the good of all its members. Each component sought its own welfare, yet contributed and was subordinated to the whole. In a world of sinful men seeking salvation, a compact society had the advantage of a readier discipline exerted by those in authority. This fact was of first importance, for men in positions of political power were, in their official capacities, limited agents of God. Those you have called to public office, Winthrop told a bumptious General Court, "have our authority from God, in way of an ordinance, such as hath the image of God eminently stamped upon it, the contempt and violation whereof hath been vindicated with examples of divine vengeance." Leaders, once selected, were to whip the moral sluggards into line, for their own good, for the welfare of society, and for the glory of God.

The variety of men's occupations made it possible for each individual to find the work in which he could best acquit himself of his obligations. But it also meant that some men were more exposed to temptation than others. Those whose work bore broadly on the welfare of others were called upon to exert a scrupulousness in their transactions commensurate with the temptation to sin. Of all private occupations trade was morally the most dangerous.

The soul of the merchant was constantly exposed to sin by virtue of his control of goods necessary to other people. Since proof of the diligence he applied in his calling was in the profits he made from precisely such exchanges, could a line be drawn between industry and avarice? The Puritans answered, as had Catholics for half a millenium, that it could, and they designated this line the "just price."

They assumed that there existed an ideal standard of valuation applicable to every situation. An unjust figure was the result not so much of the mechanical operation of an impersonal market as of some individual's gluttony. A just charge was one willingly paid by a person experienced in such matters and in need of the article but under no undue compulsion to buy. The Reverend John Cotton laid out the principles clearly: "A man may not sell above the current price, i.e., such a price as is usual in the time and place, and as another (who knows the worth of the commodity) would give for it, if he had occasion to use it. . ." A merchant's personal losses or misfortunes ought never to be reflected in an increased valuation, "but where there is a scarcity of the commodity," Cotton wrote, "there men may raise their price; for now it is a hand of God upon the commodity, and not the person." As for the particular determination of the price, in case private men cannot agree on a common estimate, "the governor, with one or more of the councell" or perhaps "certaine select men" will be able to make the matter clear. Convinced that justice could be reached, the Puritans sought only the detailed figures in concrete situations.

Equally treacherous to the soul of the businessman and the good of the public was the fact that the merchants came into control of the available supply of money and charged interest on debts. One who controlled supplies of cash or credit held a knife over a vital vein in the social body. Such a power had for centuries required the closest regulation, which it had duly received along with its rationalization in the literature on usury. But in the sixteenth century the medieval excoriation of all interest-bearing loans had given way to a qualified acceptance of interest within the limits of justice and official determination. The New England Puritans took over the continental Calvinist phrasing of this acceptance. The principle was clear. "What rule must wee observe in lending?" asked Winthrop rhetorically.

ANS: Thou must observe whether thy brother hath present or probable, or possible meanes of repayeing thee, if ther be none of these, thou must give him according to his necessity, rather then lend him as hee requires; if he hath present meanes of repayeing thee, thou art to looke at him, not as an Act of mercy, but by way of Commerce, wherein thou arte to walke by the rule of Justice. . . If any of thy brethren be poore etc. thou shalt lend him sufficient that men might not shift off this duty by the apparent hazzard. . . From him that would borrow of thee turne not away.
QUEST: What rule must wee observe in forgiveing?
ANS: Whether thou didst lend by way of Commerce or in mercy, if he have noething to pay thee [thou] must forgive him (except in cause where thou hast a surety or a lawfull pleadge) Deut. 15. 2.

John Cotton, flourishing "*Exo.* 22. 25. *Lev.* 25. 35, 36," asserted quite simply: "Noe increase to be taken of a poore brother or neighbour for anything lent unto him."

Though church and state in New England most readily impinged on the professional life of the merchant in regard to just price and usury, the assumption of justified control of economic life had a far wider applicability. If prices came under the aegis of authority so also did wages. Encouragement, even direct subsidization of economic activity, no less than restriction, flowed from the same obligation to manipulate material life for spiritual ends.

Such precepts had a special appeal to a predominantly agricultural people whose emigration was at least in part due to economic distress. Many settlers had lost their stability in a rapidly changing world where "trades are carried soe deceiptfully and unrightusly as that is almost impossible for a good upright man to maynteyne his charge and to live comfortably in his profession." The Reverend John White, who had inspired the founding of two commercial companies, voiced a typical thought in writing to Winthrop,

I heare shopkeeping begins to growe into request amongst you. In former age all kinde of retailing wares (which I confess is necessary for mens more convenient supply) was but an appendixe to some handicraft and to that I should reduce it if I were to advise in the government. Superfluity of Shopkeepers Inholders etc. are great burthens to any place. We in this Towne where I live. . .are of my knowledg at Charge *1000li* per annum in maintaining several familys in that Condition, which we might well spare for better employments wherein their labours might produce something for the common good which is not furthered by such as drawe only one from another and consequently live by the sweat of other mens brows, producing nothing themselves by their owne endevours.

At a time when mercantilism in Europe made the needs of trade a reason of state, some of these ideas of the New England leaders were archaic. Yet they were able to survive and even to flourish because the governing Fathers, being, in John Hull's phrase, "no babes nor windyheaded men," understood the necessity to found their society on a solid economic base. They merely insisted that the life of business be placed within a structure whose proportions had been drawn by the hand of God.

These ideas were put into use in the very first years of the Puritan settlements and helped shape the development of institutions and traditions from the start. Nowhere else did Calvinist doctrines of social ethics find such full application. In Geneva, Scotland, and the Netherlands theory had always to be qualified to some extent by pre-Calvinist practices. In New England, doctrine literally preceded practice. . . .

In social origins the transplanted London tradesmen were unique among the settlers. Most of the colonists had known only life on the land, either as gentlemen, independent farmers, tenants, or laborers; consequently, both the magistrates and the majority of the population brought with them the attitudes and desires of rural Englishmen. To them land meant not so much wealth as security and stability, tradition and status. Shaken out of their familiar ways by economic and political disturbances, caught up in varying degrees by the cause of religious reform, most of the 20,000 Englishmen who migrated to America in the 1630's sought to recreate the village and farm life they had known. They accepted and probably welcomed the medieval social teaching of orthodox Puritanism if only for its inspiring support of the idea of the close-knit community that existed for the good of all its members and in which each man was his brother's keeper.

For the merchants, bred in London and the bustling outports, these needs and ideas were less urgent. The great metropolis was a hot-house of new values and attitudes. In contrast to that of the average agriculturist, the life pattern of merchants who, like Thomas Savage and Robert Keayne, could boast of having received "no portion from my parents or friends to begin the world withal," and, after a career of constant striving, having emerged triumphant from financial losses "sufficient to have broken the backe of any one man in the Country"—such life patterns were characterized by geographical and social mobility. To such men the authoritarianism of Wintrhop's government, which suggested security and status to most of the settlers, tended to imply constriction and denial. Freed from the complexities and competition of the Old World cities and trained in some aspect of the production and distribution of goods, the merchants experienced a release of energies in America which frequently struck the Puritan leaders as brashness and insubordination. Conflict between men who had risen through the struggles of city life and the leaders of the Puritan Commonwealth was implicit from the start.

Yet the right of the merchants to participate fully in the community life was not challenged. All of them were received into a church and made freemen of the corporation. The difficulty took the form of a series of clashes between the merchants and the public authorities. Some of these were trivial and easily handled by the usual processes of law. Others led through subtle ways to serious trouble. In a society where theology and political theory were interwoven, thin lines of doctrine were often the threads upon which rested the justification for the use of power. Dissatisfaction with the magistracy stemming from different assumptions as to the right of self-expression, political and economic as well as religious, could be voiced in hair-splitting theological disputes. One such controversy threatened to sever the Boston merchants from the rest of the community.

The "Antinomian schism" of 1636-1637

which rocked the Bay Colony to its foundations turned on the relative importance of inner, direct religious experience and conformity to the Calvinist laws of behavior in the attainment of a Christian life. The magistracy steadfastly maintained that conformity to the letter of the law, careful performance of religious duties, was essential discipline and that it should be evident in one before he was to be admitted to church membership. To them the dissenters were dangerous mystics whose belief in the prior importance of spiritual illumination was not only a doctrinal heresy but also a threat to civil and ecclesiastical polity.

The merchants, with striking uniformity, backed the dissenters. The challenge centered in the person of Anne Hutchinson, whose husband, son, and brother-in-law were among the most prominent early merchants. Her party was composed predominantly of inhabitants of Boston, already the main seat of New England commerce. Among her adherents considered dangerous enough to be disarmed by the General Court were William, Richard, and Edward Hutchinson, Edward Rainsford, Thomas Savage, Robert Harding, Richard Parker, Edward Bendall, and John Coggeshall. Most of these merchant heretics left Massachusetts for the exile of Rhode Island, either with the Hutchinsons to Portsmouth or with William Coddington to Newport. The "Antinomian schism" uprooted some of the most flourishing merchants of Boston and prepared the soil of Rhode Island for the growth of a commercial community.

The divergence between the merchants and most of the rest of the Puritan population manifested itself more explicitly in public condemnations for malpractices in trade, particularly overcharging, usury, taking advantage of a neighbor's need. The public clamor that accompanied one such incident grew to such proportions as to indicate that an important source of discontent had been touched.

Robert Keayne was a typical self-made tradesman of London. Starting as a butcher's son in Windsor he had risen through apprenticeship in London to prominence as a merchant tailor. Transplanted to New England in 1635, he was received into the church, made a freeman of the corporation, and immediately assumed a leading position in local affairs. He moved into a house and shop on the southwest corner of Cornhill and King streets in the heart of Boston, one lot distant from the First Church and facing the central market square. Drawing on the "two or 3000 lb in good estate" he had brought with him, he reëstablished contact with his London friends and commenced his career as a retailer of imported manufactures. For four years he rode the wave of the inflation, selling badly needed goods to the immigrants for whatever prices he could get. But in November 1639 he was struck down by both church and state. Keayne was charged in General Court with "taking above six-pence in the shilling profit; in some above eight-pence; and in some small things, above two for one."

It had all started with a bag of nails he had sold at what he claimed was a perfectly reasonable price. Once this single charge had exposed the merchant to public censure, a variety of other accusations, such as overcharging for "great gold buttons," a bridle, and a skein of thread, were fired at him. Haled before the highest court he was made to face a barrage of denunciation. So agonizing were the resulting wounds that in drawing up his Last Will and Testament fourteen years later he referred again and again to the incident as if to ease the pain of that "deepe and sharpe censure that was layd upon me in the Country and carryed on with so much bitterness and indignation. . .contrary or beyond the quality and desert of the complaynts that came against me." The public ire was expressed not so much in the court's conviction of the merchant as in the fact that the fine was fixed at no less than £200. But even that was cheap considering the state of public feeling. Keayne later wrote that "if some could have had their wills they would have had the fyne mounted up to 1000lb yea 500lb was too little except some coporal punishment was added to it, such as my mans [sic] standing openly on a market day with a Bridle in his mouth or at least about his necke, as I was credibly informed. Here was well guided zeale."

So far only the civil sword had struck. The church then took up the matter. The elders studied "how farr I was guilty of all those claymors and rumors that then I lay under," and exposed his defense to a most "exquisite search." Though he escaped excommunication, a fact he later boasted of, he was given a severe admonition ". . .in the Name of the Church for selling his wares at excessive Rates, to the Dishonor of Gods name, the Offence of the Generall Cort, and the Publique scandall of the Cuntry." It took a "penetentiall acknowledgment" of his sin to regain full membership in the church.

To Keayne the most painful part of this episode (and also of his more famous involvement three years later with Goody Sherman and her sow) was not the fine or the admonition but the public insistence that he was a sinner.

> . . .the newnes and straingnes of the thing, to be brought forth into an open Court as a publique malefactor, was both a shame and an amazement to me. It was the greife of my soule (and I desire it may ever so be in a greater measure) that any act of mine (though not justly but by misconstruction) should be an occasion of scandall to the Gospell and profession of the Lord Jesus, or that my selfe should be looked at as one that had brought any just dishonor to God (which I have endeavored long and according to my weake abilitie desired to prevent) though God hath beene pleased for causes best knowne to himselfe to deny me such a blessing, and if it had beene in my owne power I should rather have chosen to have perished in my cradle than to have lived to such a time.

The merchant was as devout a Christian by his lights as his brother-in-law, the Reverend John Wilson. He had dedicated himself to the life of the spirit in the most befitting way. Not only had he been regular in his church attendance but he had kept notes on the sermons he had heard that he might refer to them later. He had studied the sacred books far into the night and left as the fruit of his labor "3 great writing bookes which are intended as an Exposition or Interpretation of the whole Bible. . .as also a 4th great writing booke which is an exposition on the Prophecy of Daniel, of the Revelations and the Prophecy of Hosea. . .all which Bookes are written with my owne hand. . .and worth all the paines and labour I have bestowed upon them, so that if I had 100lb layd me downe for them, to deprive me of them, till my sight or life should be taken of me I should not part from them." He had followed the Calvinist precepts of personal conduct. Never had he indulged in "an idle, lazie, or dronish life" or allowed himself "many spare houres to spend unprofitably away or to refresh myself with recreations." Naturally, he had prospered despite all the malice of his adversaries.

Finding evidence in the social teachings of Calvinism for the rectitude of his life, he could impute only sinfulness to those who attempted to blacken his name. But his enemies also drew upon religious ideas for the justification of their attack. To them it seemed clear that by all the relevant Calvinist standards of justice in business,

Keayne had sinned. In his scramble for profit he had trampled underfoot the notion of a just price. He had dealt with his debtors usuriously. He had put the increase of his own wealth above the common good. No amount of public benefaction could make up for such evil practices.

The original charge against the distraught merchant fell like a spark into an incendiary situation. The settlers, predisposed to believe middlemen parasites, found themselves utterly dependent on them for the most essential goods and equipment. Incapable of understanding or controlling the workings of the economy, they sought to attribute the cause of the soaring prices and the shortage of goods to human malevolence. Instances of merchants taking advantage of the situation confirmed them in their belief that only the most rigorous discipline of the businessmen could save them from misery. In the same Calvinist social teachings that had justified his life to Keayne they had a grammar for the translation of economics into morality, and in the machinery of the Puritan church and state a means of effecting these ideas. From the same texts the Puritan magistrates and the merchants read different lessons. The former learned the overwhelming importance of the organic society which subordinated the individual to the general good. Keayne learned the righteousness of those individual qualities whose secondary but attractive virtue it was to aid in the fight for success in business. Keayne's advice to the "Reverend Eldrs of this Country" that they "be as easily perswaded to yeeld in civill and earthly respects and things as they expect to prevayl with any of us when they have a request to make of us" would have implied to Winthrop the severance of the moral sinews in the body of Puritan society.

Keayne's Last Will and Testament expresses the dilemma of the first Puritan import merchants. Its 50,000 words were written under the compulsive need to gain final approval from a generation that seemed to confuse diligence with avarice. To be both a pious Puritan and a successful merchant meant to live under what would seem to have been insupportable pressures. It meant to extend to the life of business a religious enthusiasm which must be continuously dampened lest it singe the corners of another's life. It meant to accumulate as much wealth as one righteously could, only to dispose of it, like a steward, according to the principle *uti non frui*. It demanded against the natural desire to live spontaneously and heedlessly the total rationalization of life. Above all, it required an amount of self-discipline that only great faith could sustain.

Only a short time after New England was settled, the ministers began to complain that the religious zeal of the colonists was diminishing. A decline from the intense piety of the founders was probably inevitable; yet "declension" also meant that far-reaching changes were taking place in the Holy Commonwealth. One of these was the "Half-Way Covenant," another the founding of the Brattle Street Church, both of which are described in this selection by HERBERT W. SCHNEIDER (1892-), professor of religion at Claremont Graduate School. He explains these and other changes as reflections of a broader shift in the religious sensibility of the colonists, their "loss of the sense of sin."°

A Changing Sense of Sin

. . .Puritan thrift soon produced Yankee prosperity, and Yankee prosperity produced urban aristocracies. The precariousness of the frontier gave place to the security of the towns. Luxury gradually crept in. The younger generations could afford to rest a bit on their fathers' oars. They had not undergone the moral discipline of the frontier. They did not realize what it cost to found New England. To them New England was home, not a howling wilderness. Consequently their fathers' strenuous standards began to irritate them, and the philosophy of God's wonder-working providence began to take on a hollow sound. But if the children complained of the severity of their fathers, the fathers complained of the worldliness of their children. No one willingly sees his offspring consume what he has laboriously produced, even though he may have produced it for that very purpose. The early standards were accordingly preached to the youth and upheld as inherently worthy of obedience; their original practical value being less conspicuous, they were enforced by religious sanctions. Prohibitions were made and restraining laws enacted. Waste of time became inherently bad and diversions became sins by divine commandment.

Cotton Mather, for example, declared:

 Footnotes omitted.

"The general rules, which in all recreations are to be observed, are so generally transgressed in these games [of cards or dice] that ordinarilly it can be no other than a sin to use them. These diversions fascinate the minds of those that practice them, at such a rate, that if ever those persons come to be converted unto God, they bitterly lament the loss of time in which that practice hath involved them. And the many other passions and follies almost inseparable from these diversions, render the diversions themselves to be sins against the commandments, which prohibit the evils thereby occasioned."

In 1653, the General Court at Boston was aroused to action. "Upon information of sundry abuses and misdemeanors committed by several persons on the Lord's Day, not only by children playing in the streetes and other places, but by youthes, maydes, and other persons, both straungers and others, uncivilly walkinge the streetes and feilds, travilling from towne to towne, goeing on ship-board, frequentinge common houses and other places to drinke, sport, and otherwise to mispend that precious time, which thinges tend much to the dishonor of God, the reproach of religion, and the prophanation of his holy Sabbath, the sanctification whereof is sometime put for all dutyes immediately respectinge the service of God conteined in the first table; it is therefore ordered by this Court and the authoritie, that no children, youths, maydes, or other persons shall transgress in the like kind on penalty of beinge reputed great provokers of the high displeasure of Almighty God, and further incurringe the penaltyes hereafter expressed."

Even the ministers, though they railed against worldliness, were infected with pride in their worldly prosperity. Note, for example, the exultant worldliness ill-concealed in this defense of religion: "When the Lord stirred up the spirits of so many of his people to come over into this wilderness, it was not for Worldly Wealth, or a better livelihood for the outward man. The generality of the people that came over, professed the contrary: Nor had we any rational grounds to expect such a thing in such a wilderness. Tho' God hath blessed his poor people here, and there are that have increased here, from small beginnings to great estates; That the Lord may call this whole generation to witness.—O Generation see! Look upon your towns and fields, Look upon your habitations and shops, and ships, and behold your numerous posterity, and great increase in the blessings of the Land and Sea; Have I been a wilderness unto you? We must needs answer, No, Lord, Thou hast been a gracious God, and exceeding good unto thy servants, even in these earthly blessings; we live in a more plentiful and comfortable manner than ever we did expect."

The older clergy were thus placed more and more on the defensive. They bewailed the degenerate times. "As to New England's First Ways: What glorious things might be spoken to the praise of free grace. But O! what a sad metamorphosis hath there of later years past upon these churches and plantations?—It must be spoken in the name of the Lord, O New England, Thy God expects better things from thee and thy children; not worldliness;—not an itching after new things and ways;—not a drawing loose in the yoke of God? Alas! How is New-England, in danger of being lost even in New-England?"

In the Cambridge Platform of 1648, it had been agreed that children of members of the Church Covenant of Grace were also members. [1] However, these members by

[1] The Cambridge Platform was the formal definition of Congregational church structure written by

birth, when they came of age, were expected to make public profession of personal regeneration before they were admitted to the Holy Communion. When the time came, many of this second generation did not make such a personal profession; nevertheless they not only regarded themselves as full members, but asked to have their children baptised. This brought the issue to a head. Had the churches yielded to this demand, the great majority of the third generation of church members, no doubt, would have been unregenerate. Had the church not yielded at all, and insisted that even the second generation should be excluded from the church unless they professed regeneration, the churches would have lost many of their younger and most influential members. In either case the Holy Commonwealth was doomed. In this dilemma, which was debated in the Ministerial Convention of 1657 and the Synod of 1662, the decision to compromise was finally reached. The unregenerate second generation were allowed to remain in church and to have their children baptised into the church; but neither they nor their children were allowed to become partakers of the Lord's Supper—they were said to be members, but not in full communion. This was the famous Half-Way Covenant which the churches were compelled to adopt in practice, though several generations of theologians, as we shall see, struggled in vain to justify it in theory.

The chief stumbling-block in the whole question was the practice of exacting public relations of the regenerating work of grace, before a person could claim divine election and membership in the Covenant of Grace. Rather than undergo this ordeal, which was usually both embarrassing and stultifying, sinners were content to remain in their natural state and forego the privileges of communion. Thus, within a comparatively short time, the churches were composed, for the most part, of technically unregenerate persons, known as baptised adult non-communicants. All parties usually accepted this state of affairs in good humor, as a sensible evasion of an issue which, if insisted upon, would only have made everybody uncomfortable.

The first serious threat to the Half-Way Covenant came in 1698, when a group of wealthy and influential trustees of Harvard College, who had incurred the hostility of President Increase Mather, revolted and organized an independent church in Brattle Street, Boston. In this group was Thomas Brattle, whose father was one of the wealthiest men in New England, and who, himself, was a prosperous business-man. He had spent several years in England after his graduation from Harvard and was strongly inclined toward the Anglican type of worship. He was an astronomer and mathematician. In 1692, he had opposed the witchcraft scare in which Increase Mather was involved. His brother, William Brattle, was minister at Cambridge and a tutor at Harvard. In his church the public relation of experiences was discontinued about the year 1696; and, though he raised no theological issues in his sermons which his fellow-ministers could dispute, he emphasized increasingly the practical moral problems of the day and the idea of God's great mercy. These two brothers, together with John Leverett (later President of Harvard), gathered around them some very respectable and prosperous citizens of Boston, as well as several other members of Harvard College; they built a church in Brattle Square and invited Benjamin Colman to be their minister. Colman was a Harvard graduate who had been preaching in nonconformist churches in England since 1695. On the advice of the Brattle Street group, he arranged to be ordained by the

---

the ministers in New England at a synod in Cambridge, Massachusetts.—Ed.

Presbytery in London before returning to Boston. He arrived, therefore, fully ordained and completely independent of the Boston Association controlled by Increase Mather, and the church was thus a direct challenge to the New England theocracy. The "undertakers of the New Church" immediately issued a Manifesto which contained, among others, the following principles: (1) Loyalty was pledged to the Westminster Confession. (2) Selections from the Scriptures were to be read without comment by the minister. (3) Baptism was to be administered, not only to "such as professed faith and obedience to Christ and to their children," but also to the children of "any professed Christians" who engaged to educate the children in the Christian religion. (4) Communion might be received only by "persons of visible sanctity," and the pastor was responsible for ascertaining such sanctity. (5) "But we assume not to ourselves to impose upon any a public relation of their experiences." (6) If any fell into "scandalous sin" they might be excommunicated by the pastor with the consent of the brethren. (7) "A particular church is a society of Christians by mutual agreement." (8) All baptised persons, women, as well as men, who contributed to the maintenance of the church, were to have a vote in electing the minister. [2]

This Manifesto caused a sensation among the ministers. Increase Mather attempted to force the authors to retract it, and, when he failed, he wrote a vigorous pamphlet, *The Order of the Gospel, Professed and Practiced by the Churches of Christ in New England, Justified.* The ministers of Salem wrote a long letter of advice in which they urged the Brattle Street men to read a famous pamphlet, *Spiritual Milk for Boston Babes drawn out of the Breasts of both Testaments*; they condemned them for the self-confident and arrogant way in which they had disregarded the other churches and their disciplines; they accused them of laxity in the matters of communion, public relations, and baptism; and they concluded by stating that "the females are certainly more than the males and consequently the choice of ministers is put into their hands. . . .It is certain the baptized adult non-communicants in most if not all the assemblies in the land, are more than the communicants, and consequently, if they should take their rule and manners from this article [of the Manifesto], they might make worse work in all the churches than we are willing to say." And someone contributed "a simple poem upon the authors and their design" which concluded:

"Our churches turn genteel:
"Our parsons grow trim and trig,
"With wealth, wine and wig
"And their heads are covered with meal."

These documents reveal quite clearly what was happening, not only in Brattle Street, but also throughout New England. The genteel churches were turning from the gospel of election and regeneration; they were content to be simply "societies of Christians by mutual agreement"; and to be Christians meant merely to "profess faith in and obedience to Christ" and to avoid "scandalous sin." In other words, these respectable Yankees wished thenceforth to be known as Christians, not as unregenerates. Yet all this growing pride could be accompanied by lip-service to the Westminster Confession and the doctrine of depravity. The theory remained intact, though the sinners disappeared.

[2] These eight principles, with the exception of the first, were contrary to the procedures established in the Cambridge Platform. According to the Platform, baptism was limited to children of church members; the Lord's Supper was administered only to persons who made a "public relation" of their conversion experiences before the church; and power to elect the minister rested with the men who partook of Communion.—Ed.

The Brattle Street church issue, however, still left the question of communion in the old embarrassing form. The responsibility for determining visible sanctity was shifted from the participant himself to the minister, but theoretically the sacrament of communion could not be administered so liberally as that of baptism. And in general the ministers believed that their "main duty was to communicants." To meet this situation, the Reverend Solomon Stoddard, of Northampton, revised the theory of the communion. In his *Doctrine of Instituted Churches* (1700), the theory was developed that the Lord's Supper was not primarily a sacred privilege of the elect, but a means of salvation, and should therefore be administered to the unregenerate provided they were of good conversation. He answered boldly to the question: "Whether such persons as have a good conversation and a competent knowledge, may come to the Lords Supper, with a good conscience, in case they know themselves to be in a natural condition? Answ. They may and ought to come tho they know themselves to be in a natural condition; this ordinance is instituted for all the adult members of the Church who are not scandalous, and therefore must be attended by them; as no man may neglect prayer, or hearing the Word, because he cannot do it in faith, so he may not neglect the Lords Supper."

Increase Mather came to the rescue of the traditional theory in his *Order of the Gospel*; and in reply to it, Stoddard further developed his theory by saying: "This Ordinance has a proper tendency in its own to convert men. Herein men may learn the necessity and sufficiency of the death of Christ in order to Pardon. Here is an affecting offer of Christ crucifyed; here is a sealing of the Covenant, that if men come to Christ, they shall be saved, which is a great means to convince of safety in coming to Christ. All Ordinances are for the saving good of those that they are to be administered unto. This Ordinance is according to Institution to be applyed to visible Saints, though Unconverted, therefore it is for their saving good, and consequently for their conversion." And he defined visible saints as "Such as make a serious profession of the true religion, together with those that do descend from them, till rejected of God."

Stoddardeanism spread rapidly among the younger clergy and in the wealthier churches, in spite of the efforts of such influential opponents as the Mathers. These smug ministers of God still maintained their divine right to govern the affairs of the colony, though the revocation of the Massachusetts charter, in 1692, had put an official end to the theocracy. Cotton Mather's *Magnalia Christi Americana* was, even at the time of its publication in 1702, little more than a ponderous monument erected over a dead cause. Yet the champions lingered on, apparently unaware of the moral and intellectual revolution going on about them. Cotton Mather, to be sure, made a desperate stand; he proposed to form Societies for the Reformation of Manners and for the Suppression of Vice. He outlined the following "Points of consideration, which may be read to the societies, at their meetings, from time to time, with a proper pause after each of them, that any member may offer what he pleases upon it. 1. Is there any remarkable disorder in the place, which requires our endeavours for the suppression of it?. . . 2. Is there any particular person, whose disorderly behaviour may be so scandalous, that it may be proper to send him our charitable admonition? Or, Are there any contending persons whom we should exhort to quench their contentions? 3. Is there any particular service to the interests of religion, which we may conveniently request our ministers to take notice of? 4. Is there anything which we may do well to mention and recommend to the magistrates, for the further promotion of good order? 5. Is there any sort of officers among us who are so unmindful of their duty, that we may properly remind them of it? 6. Can any further methods be devised that ignorance and wickedness may be chased from our people in general; and that domestic piety, in particular, may flourish among them? 7. Is there any instance of oppression or fraudulence in the dealings of any sort of people, which may call for our efforts to prevent it in future? 8. Is there any matter to be humbly recommended to the legislative power, to be enacted into law for the public benefit? 9. Do we know of any person languishing under heavy affliction, and what can we do for the succour of that afflicted neighbour? 10. Has any person a proposal to make, for the further advantage, assistance, and usefulness of this society?"

This final attempt at universal prohibition was, of course, a vain effort to awaken in others a sense of sin which was quite lacking in the Mathers themselves. Being better than others, they tried in vain to make others better. In the end they became a laughing-stock, entertaining the public by heaping invectives on their critics. Increase Mather died in 1723, and Cotton Mather in 1728, both sour old men, persecuted persecutors; and with them died the last and most pompous incarnations of the political theocracy.

The final blow at the Mather dynasty came from John Wise, and ushered in a new philosophy. Both the Rev. Colman, of Brattle Street, and the Rev. Stoddard, of Northampton, were conservative Presbyterians in the sense that they favored centralized church government, and the reforms which they advocated were in the interests of making the policies of the churches more palatable to an unregenerate generation of highly respectable laymen. They were quite willing to sacrifice the idea of the Holy Commonwealth for the sake of the prosperity of the churches. And nothing would have suited them better than a national church comfortably established in the Commonwealth of New England.

. . .Increase Mather had been one of those responsible for calling the Synod of 1679-80 to consider measures that "may appear necessary for the preventing of schisms, heresies, profaneness and the establishment of the churches in one faith and order of the gospel." In 1691 he attempted a union of the New England churches with the Presbyterians. In 1700 the Massachusetts clergy, under the leadership of Solomon Stoddard, formed a plan for a "national church," and in 1705 they adopted a system of associations and standing councils. In 1708 the Connecticut clergy adopted the Saybrook Platform, which provided Consociations, or local presbyteries. A similar move was expected in Boston. This was the signal for revolt on the part of the strict Congregationalists. In 1710, John Wise, of the Second Church of Ipswich, published *The Churches Quarrel Espoused*, and in 1717, his famous *Vindication of the Government of the New England Churches*. These tracts might have been merely restatements of the traditional Congregational theory, as it had been expressed in John Cotton's *Way of Congregational Churches Cleared*, or as it was restated later (1738) in Samuel Mather's *Apology for the Liberties of the Churches in New England*. But coming at this juncture, both the internal argument and the external application were radically changed. The other tracts were defenses of American churches against Anglican authority; John Wise's tracts were defenses of particular congregations against their own clergy. The conventional argument was based on the Dutch theology of primitive Christian democracy; John Wise's, on the ideas of natural law and civil liberty. The former Congregationalism was an integral part of the philosophy of the Holy Commonwealth; John Wise's Congregationalism was the first formulation of secular republicanism.

John Wise was no ordinary clergyman. He had been jailed for obstructing the collection of the royal taxes. He had been a fighting chaplain in the expedition against Quebec, and he later wrote a plea for paper currency. He had been contaminated, while at Harvard, by the new books in the library, and among them especially by Pufendorf's *De Iure Naturae et Gentium*; and the legal theories which he gleaned from this work became the groundwork of his defense of democracy in the churches. "It seems most agreeable with the light of nature, that if there be any of the regular government settled in the church of God, it must needs be a democracy. This is a form of government which the light of nature does highly value, and often directs to as most agreeable to the just and natural prerogatives of human beings. . . . A man in making himself a subject, he alters himself from a freeman into a slave, which to do is repugnant to the law of nature. Also the natural equality of men amongst men must be duly favored; in that government was never established by God or nature, to give one man a prerogative to insult over another. . . . Honor all men. The end of all good government is to cultivate humanity, and promote the happiness of all, and the good of every man in all his rights, his life, liberty, estate, honor, etc., without injury or abuse done to any." Then he goes on to prove that the New England congregations can be justified on the basis of these ideas.

Here we have a complete reversal of Puritan philosophy. The state is not justified because it makes a contribution to the Kingdom of God; the churches of God are justified because they tend to "cultivate humanity and promote the happiness of all and the good of every man in all his rights." Nothing could be a more eloquent tribute to the new spirit in New England: the churches are to be modelled on the principles of civil society, not *vice versa.* It is not the concept of democracy which is significant here, for that had been present from the beginning of New England; it is the secularization of democracy, the dethronement of God, the unholiness of the commonwealth, that marks a revolution.

Had this been merely an attack on the Mathers and their Presbyterianism, the tract would have been buried with the Mathers; but, since it was really the beginning of a new religion, it was printed and reprinted, read and re-read, until by 1772 its re-publication transformed it into one of the bibles of the American Revolution. The Puritan sense of sin had yielded to what Samuel Mather called the liberty of the laity.

The heart of Puritanism was its conception of the church. Revolting against "Popish remnants" in the Church of England, the Puritans developed a new theory of the church as a group of individuals identified as "saints." This theory was first applied in practice by the founders of New England. The early history of this conception of the church, its adoption by the colonists, and its subsequent history in New England are described by EDMUND S. MORGAN (1916-) in *Visible Saints: The History of a Puritan Idea.* The climax of his story is the invention of the Half-Way Covenant, a device that significantly altered the standards for church membership originally established in New England. What reasons does Morgan suggest to explain the introduction of the Half-Way Covenant?*

The Half-Way Covenant Reconsidered

The English emigrants to New England were the first Puritans to restrict membership in the church to visible saints, to persons, that is, who had felt the stirrings of grace in their souls, and who could demonstrate this fact to the satisfaction of other saints. The early Separatists had demanded the exclusion from the church of the visibly wicked; the later Separatists, and especially Henry Ainsworth, had implied that the exclusion of the wicked meant the inclusion only of saints; and at the same time the nonseparating English Puritan divines had been teaching their readers and listeners how to recognize the movements of grace within the soul and thus to determine whether one was a saint or not. It had remained for the New Englanders to combine and carry these ideas to fruition by constructing their churches entirely of persons who had demonstrated their sainthood to one another.

The impulse that produced this development was not novel. It had moved Donatists, Montanists, Albigensians, and many other Christians over the centuries. In the sixteenth and seventeenth centuries it carried the Baptists and the Quakers even farther than the Puritans. It was nothing more than man's yearning for holiness. The church has always been man's way of approaching divinity, and those who have joined the church have often sought to carry it with them in their

*Reprinted from Edmund S. Morgan, *Visible Saints: The History of a Puritan Idea* (New York: New York University Press, 1963). Footnotes omitted.

progress from the wickedness of the world toward the goodness of God. The danger in such a move is seldom apparent to those who make it, the danger of deserting the world in search of a perfection that belongs only to heaven.

Those Puritans who believed in Congregationalism, that is, in churches gathered from the world by free consent, were especially prone to the danger. Although they prided themselves on not seeking perfection, the very act of gathering a church implied a departure from the world and a closer approach to perfection than others had attained. In New England the requirement that members have saving faith moved the churches farther from the world than the Separatist ones in England and Holland, which had required only good behavior and orthodox belief. To be sure, the New England Puritans admitted that their churches inevitably contained bad men as well as good, hypocrites who deceived their brethren and perhaps themselves by false assurance. But no such persons were knowingly tolerated. As Thomas Shepard, the pastor of the church at Cambridge, said, "if we could be so Eagle-eyed, as to discern them now that are Hypocrites, we should exclude them now," for "one man or woman secretly vile, which the Church hath not used all means to discover, may defile a whole Church."

In moving their churches so close to God and so far from the world, the New England Puritans were doing what they believed that God required. But the move created a special difficulty for them, which was closely related to the problem that I have elsewhere called the Puritan dilemma, the problem of doing right in a world that does wrong. In a study of John Winthrop I have tried to show how an individual Puritan met this dilemma and how it affected his conduct of the civil government of Massachusetts. John Winthrop, while trying to live as God required, learned that he must live *in* the world, face its temptations, and share its guilt; and Winthrop helped to prevent the government of Massachusetts from seeking a greater perfection in this world than God required or allowed.

Winthrop had less control, and less understanding, of the church than of the state. And the church, by any standards, had to be more pure than the state. But the New England churches, by the mid-1630's, were committed to a degree of purity that left their relationship with the world highly uncertain and untried by any previous experience in England or Europe. If the church could have been truly gathered from the world into eternity, there would have been no problem, for in eternity the visible and invisible churches would have become one. Freed from the world, and from their own corruptions, the members could have adored God in perpetual glory. But the visible church, like man himself, must remain *in* the world and must not only bring its members closer to God but must also help to redeem the rest of the world.

It was the church's task, acknowledged by Christians in all ages, to spread the gospel, to offer to all men the means of salvation. Though Puritans and other Calvinists thought the means would be effective only with God's predestined elect, not even the New England churches could hope to identify God's elect *before* God made that election manifest in saving faith. Though the New England churches might accept for membership only those who already had saving faith, they must offer the means of faith indiscriminately to all, serving as God's instrument for begetting faith in those who were predestined to receive it but had not yet done so. How to discharge this basic responsibility of the church became an increasingly difficult problem for the New England Puritans as they developed their idea of restricted church membership: their churches must not only be gathered out of the world but must continually gather *in* the world, continually search for new saints. . . .

When they left England in the 1630's, many Puritans assumed that they could and would leave the bad part of the world behind. They soon found that they could not. The fifteen or twenty thousand men and women who disembarked in New England between 1630 and 1640 included large numbers who had to be classified as visibly wicked, so many indeed that some of the founders contemplated a further withdrawal to an isolated area from which this "mixed multitude" should be excluded. The wisest recognized that the world neither could nor should be left behind, and no further exodus occurred. But in the 1630's, by adopting the new strict view of church membership, the New England Puritans executed a spiritual withdrawal from the mixed multitude that amounted almost to an ecclesiastical abdication from the world. They failed to consider, before adopting the new standards of membership, what relation their churches should bear to the mass of men excluded by those standards, and their failure exposed them to even more serious charges of neglect and arrogance than they themselves had formerly made against the Separatists.

Outside the church in New England stood not only the mixed multitude of wicked Englishmen and heathen natives, but also the visibly good, who understood and believed the doctrines of Christianity and lived accordingly but who lacked the final experience of grace. The New England churches made no differentiation among these seemingly different men. Indeed the New England ministers devoted a good deal of time to showing that there was no difference in the eyes of God between the vilest sinner and the "civil" man, who obeyed God's commands outwardly but did not love God in his heart. The only distinction among men in the eyes of God was between those who had saving faith and those who lacked it. Therefore the civil and the uncivil alike were kept outside God's church.

Outside the church in New England, moreover, a man was much farther removed from most of the means of grace than he would have been in the Old World. In England and Holland the establishment of Separatist churches had deprived no one of church membership, for the Separatists were surrounded by other, more comprehensive churches open to all. In New England the Puritans, certain that their way was the only one, forbade the erection of other churches. If a man could not qualify as a visible saint, he was wholly outside any church. He could not be baptized. He could not have his children baptized. He could not take communion. In England both these ordinances were available to everyone and were widely believed to be means of conversion through which God acted on the individual just as He did through preaching of the Gospel. But the New England Puritans did not share this belief and therefore felt obliged to deny baptism and communion to the unconverted. In their view both ordinances were seals of the covenant of grace which God extended to his elect. To permit an unbeliever to participate in them would be blasphemous. By this exclusion, however, the church deprived itself of two traditional means of bringing unregenerated men closer to God.

Church discipline, which might also have served this purpose, was similarly confined to those who least needed it. It was used only for recovering or expelling backsliding members. In England, though church discipline was lax, everyone in the community was subject to it. But the New England Puritans assigned to the state the task of disciplining those whom they excluded from their churches.

The absence of ties between the unregenerate part of the community and the church gave the latter an unprecedented purity, but it also placed the very life of the church in jeopardy. The members of the New England churches had themselves come from imperfect churches, in which they had learned the doctrines of Christianity, had taken the sacraments, and received the experience of grace that qualified them for membership in the proper churches of New England. But how would the mass of men who had come to New England unqualified for membership ever become qualified? How would civil men be encouraged to persevere in their outward obedience in the hope of eventual faith? How would the wicked be shown their wickedness? How would the gospel be spread to the heathen? Before leaving for America, many Puritan spokesmen had affirmed a desire to convert the natives. How would they do it with a church designed only for the saved? Without a surrounding of imperfect, unreformed churches, where would the reformed ones obtain a supply of members? How would God's elect be plucked from the mixed multitude?

New Englanders had failed to consider these questions, and when English Puritans asked them, the New Englanders, like the Separatists before them, replied in terms that exposed their failure to recognize the church's mission in the world. John Cotton, for example, the principal spokesman for the New England way, could only ask of his critics: "May there not fall out to be Hypocrites in our Flock? and must wee not preach for their conversion? And are not the children of the Members of our Church, many of them such, as when they grow up stand in need of converting grace? . . .Besides when an Indian or unbeleever commeth into the Church, doe not all the prophets that preach the Word. . .apply their speech to his conviction and conversion?"

The honest answer to the last of these questions was probably no. Nevertheless the New England Puritans did take one measure to fulfill the church's evangelical mission. Instead of waiting for unbelievers to wander into the meetinghouse, the civil government of Massachusetts in 1646 passed a law requiring everyone within a town to attend the preaching of the word. Such laws were also passed in the New Haven and Connecticut colonies. The government undoubtedly hoped that compulsory church attendance would improve the colonists not only in godliness but in behavior. Whether the result matched the hope is questionable, for those who attended from compulsion were unlikely to derive from the experience any feeling of kinship to the church. New England preaching, from the point of view of the unregenerate, left much to be desired. Although the Puritans acknowledged preaching to be the principal means through which God converted men, ministers addressed themselves more to saints than to sinners, in sermons designed less to plant the seed of faith than to nourish it where it already grew.

To be sure, not all ministers neglected the unregenerate. Some preachers undoubtedly tried to make new converts from their captive audiences. The surviving sermons of Thomas Hooker, for example, are often addressed to perishing sinners. A few ministers like John Eliot even devoted their spare time to converting the Indians. But for the most part the New England churches, in striving for purity of membership, neglected sinners and heathen and civil men to concentrate on the advancement in grace of those who had already demonstrated saving faith.

If a New Englander did pause to consider the sinners outside the church, he was likely to compromise his insistence on purity of membership. John Eliot, for example, in corresponding with English Puritans about the church's evangelical mission, found himself proposing measures that were inconsistent with New England practice. At one point he advocated admitting everyone in a congregation to the privileges of the church "so as to keep the whole heape of chaff and corne together, only excluding the ignorant and prophane and scandalous." From this undifferentiated mass, there might be simultaneously gathered a special group of "the holy Saints, who are called higher by the grace of Christ," and who might "injoy together a more strickt and select communion" without deserting the regular parochial communion. At another time Eliot proposed transplanting the holiest members of outstanding congregations into other congregations which needed some shining examples to leaven the wicked in their midst.

Eliot never attempted to carry out these novel proposals which he made to Richard Baxter as suggestions for the churches of England. In New England, he and other Puritan ministers continued to exclude from the sacraments all but the proven regenerate. In spite of prodding from English Presbyterians and Anglicans, the New Englanders refused to reverse their withdrawal from the world, and refused any accommodation within the church to the well meaning and well behaved. But the world has its own ways of controlling those who propel themselves too far from it; and the New England churches were eventually brought back to earth, not by the corruptions of the flesh, but by its biology.

The way of the world even in Massachusetts was to be born, grow old, and die. In the process each generation had to beget the next; and children did not spring full-grown and fully educated from their mothers' wombs. The had to be nursed and nurtured mentally and spiritually as well as physically until they were fit to stand by themselves. Somehow the organization of the church had to be accommodated to these facts of life. As the saints died and their children grew up, there had to be a way of getting the new generation into the church.

The Baptists, with a yearning for purity similar to that of the Puritans, solved the problem, or succeeded in ignoring it, by recruiting all new members from adult Christians who had been awakened by Baptist preaching or the preaching of other ministers. As old believers died, newly converted ones would take their places; children were incapable of any kind of membership. The Puritans, both Separatist and non-Separatist, had disclaimed "Anabaptism." Although the most ardent sometimes succumbed to its attractions, the great majority believed that God required the church to baptize not only converted saints previously unbaptized but also the children of saints. Such children became members of the church, but not in the same sense as their parents.

In what sense was a question that troubled the Separatists in England and Holland very little. The younger children of Separatist church members there did not participate in the Lord's Supper, but as they grew to maturity, they could easily qualify for all the privileges of the church, if they wished to, simply by behaving themselves and learning what they were taught. But the Separatist experience could offer no assistance to New Englanders in this matter. New England had prescribed not merely understanding and good behavior but an experience of conversion, an experience beyond the range of human volition, as a qualification for adult membership. Yet New England still admitted children to this church by baptism, apparently expecting that they would pass from child membership to adult membership when they grew up, just as they had done in the Separatist churches and in the Church of England. It was an arrogant and inconsistent expectation, for it implied a presumption that every child of a saint was destined for salvation and such a presumption was obviously wrong. No Christian could believe that grace was really hereditary.

The Puritans tried to overcome this inconsistency by demanding that when the child of a saint grew up he must demonstrate to the church that he was indeed saved. Until he did so, by the same kind of examination that adults seeking membership were subjected to, he should not be admitted to the Lord's Supper. So said John Cotton, Richard Mather, and the synod of divines who between 1646 and 1648 drafted the exposition of Puritan beliefs and practices which is usually referred to as the Cambridge Platform. But the men who framed the Cambridge Platform did not say what happened to the membership of a child if he grew up and did not experience faith.

Before two decades had passed, the fact was plain that most children of saints did not receive saving faith by the time they were physically mature. To judge from surviving records, it was uncommon for a man or woman to have the requisite religious experience before he was in his twenties. Often it came much later, and many otherwise good men and women never received it.

But if the holy spirit reached these men and women late or not at all, biological urges reached them early. They married young and had large families. When an unconverted child of a church member produced a child of his own, the minister of his church was presented with a problem, the complexity of which had not been foreseen by the architects of the New England system. The new father (or mother) had been in some sense a member of the church. Was he still? If so, was he a member in a different sense than before? What about the child? Was the child a member? Should the child be baptized?

The questions were difficult to answer, because every answer generated several more questions. If a child who grew to physical maturity without receiving faith was to be considered no longer a member of the church, how and when should his expulsion take place? The fact that he had acquired a child before he acquired faith was no sign that he would not eventually attain faith. Should the church meanwhile cast him out? If so, upon what grounds could it be done? The New Englanders, in adopting the new standard of membership, had not correspondingly altered their conception of church discipline. Admonitions and excommunications were still applied only for misconduct or for openly expressed heretical ideas; no one suggested that anyone be excommunicated for failure to display signs of saving faith. When, therefore, a child of a member grew to maturity without faith but without misconduct, it was impossible to find grounds for expelling him. To excommunicate him for having a child in lawful wedlock was palpably absurd. On the other hand, if he remained a member, his child must be entitled to baptism, and if so, why not that child's child too, and so on until the church should cease to be a company of the faithful and should become a genealogical society of the descendants of the faithful.

The Puritans had in fact moved the church so far from the world that it would no longer fit the biological facts of life. Had they been willing to move it a little farther still, by forming monasteries instead of churches, they might have concentrated on their own purity and left to others the task of supplying the church with new members. Had they been willing to abandon infant baptism, they might at least have avoided the embarrassment of trying to adjust spiritual growth to physical. As it was, they had chosen to apply in time and space a conception of the church that could never fit those dimensions. Given both infant baptism and the restriction of church membership to visible saints, it was impossible for the Puritans either to evade the questions just posed or to answer them without an elaborate casuistry that bred dissatisfaction and disagreement. The history of the New England churches during the seventeenth and eighteenth centuries was in large measure a history of these dissatisfactions and disagreements.

In the first decade after the establishment of the more rigorous standard of membership, the questions were not yet urgent. The older children of church members in the new churches had been baptized in England and were perhaps not considered as sharing in their parents' membership. By the late 1640's, however, an increasing number of children who had been baptized in New England churches were coming of age without a religious experience and starting families of their own. The synod which met at Cambridge in 1646-1648 had been asked to decide the status of these persons. Since it failed to do so, every church during the 1650's had to face the question for itself, and most of them seem to have adopted a do-nothing policy by neither expelling the second-generation adults nor baptizing their third-generation children.

By the late 1650's, the preaching of the word was generating few conversions, and with the end of the Great Migration, the overseas supply of saints had been cut off. As the first generation of Puritans died, the churches declined rapidly in membership, and it appeared that a majority of the population would soon be unbaptized. This was an alarming situation for a community which had been founded for religious puposes. It was one thing to create a church of saints; it was another to let those saints carry the church out of the world with them entirely when they died. A meeting of ministers in 1657 and a full-scale synod in 1662 considered the problem and tried to find a solution that would retain a pure membership without destroying the church.

The synod did not address itself to the fundamental problem of the church's relation to the world at large, the problem of how to convert the unconverted. Instead, it confined itself to the more limited question posed by the birth of children to baptized persons who had not or not yet received saving faith. The synod adopted seven propositions, most of which simply affirmed the prevailing New England ideas about infant baptism and the construction of churches from visible saints. But the third, fourth, and fifth propositions settled the problem of the unconverted members and their children, as follows:

> Proposition 3d. The Infant-seed of confederate visible Believers, are members of the same Church with their parents, and when grown up, are personally under the Watch, Discipline and Government of that Church.
>
> Proposition 4th. These Adult persons are not therefore to be admitted to full Communion, meerly because they are and continue

members, without such further qualifications, as the Word of God requireth thereunto.

Proposition 5th. Church-members who were admitted in minority, understanding the Doctrine of Faith, and publickly professing their assent thereto; not scandalous in life, and solemnly owning the Covenant before the Church, wherein they give up themselves and their Children to the Lord, and subject themselves to the Government of Christ in the Church, their Children are to be Baptized.

The fifth proposition was the crucial one. It meant that if a person born and baptized in the church did not receive faith he could still continue his membership and have his own children baptized, by leading a life free of scandal, by learning and professing the doctrines of Christianity, and by making a voluntary submission to God and His church. This submission, which proposition five calls "owning" the covenant, involved acknowledging the covenant with Christ and the church that had been made for one in infancy by one's parents, acknowledging, that is, so far as it lay within human power to do so. Although Puritan theology made such an acknowledgment meaningless unless it was the product of saving faith, owning the covenant was not intended to imply the genuine participation in the covenant of grace that came from saving faith. Nor was "understanding the Doctrine of Faith" supposed to imply the actual possession of faith. All the actions prescribed by the fifth proposition could be performed without saving faith. All were designed for the well-meaning, well-behaved but faithless offspring of the faithful. By the fifth proposition, these persons could retain their membership in the pure churches of New England simply by fulfilling the conditions which had formerly been required for membership in the Separatist churches of England and Holland.

The membership they retained, however, was not the full membership that had been granted in the Separatist churches. Rather it was the continuation of the membership they had had as children: they could not vote in church affairs, and they could not participate in the Lord's Supper (they were not members in "full communion"). What they gained was two privileges which had probably been hitherto denied them in most New England churches: the application of church discipline (they could be admonished or excommunicated for bad conduct) and baptism for their children. They were "half-way" members, and the synod's whole solution to the question of their status was dubbed the "half-way covenant." . . .

New England piety may have been declining, but the halfway covenant was *not* a symptom of decline. Rather it was an attempt to answer questions which neither English Puritans nor Separatists had had to face, questions which were created by New England's rigorous new conception of church membership but which the originators of that concept, during their brief experience, had generally been able to evade. By the 1660's the questions could no longer be evaded, but if the clergy and members of the New England churches had really been less pious than their predecessors, those questions might never have arisen. If, for example, they had succumbed to Arminianism, it would have been possible for anyone who wished to do so to join the church, simply by affirming his possession of a faith that lay within the reach of human volition. The halfway covenant became necessary, because New England churches of the second generation did hold to the standards of the first, because they did retain the belief in infant baptism, and because they did insist on the pattern of conversion outlined by Perkins and Hildersam and Ames.

Whether there was a decline of piety in

the population at large is another question entirely, for the halfway covenant had nothing to do with the population at large. It is not a question I am prepared to settle, but it may be worth pointing out that though the rate of conversions during the second and third decades of New England's history was probably much lower than the founders had anticipated, this was not necessarily a sign of a decline in piety. The bulk of the population had arrived during the Great Migration of the 1630's and probably a large number of the first church members became so before the new admissions system was completely set up. How many would have become members if they had had to pass the new test we cannot tell. Since the second generation of New Englanders was thus actually the first generation in which every church member did have to pass the new test, a comparison of membership statistics in the first few decades, if they were available, would not solve our problem.

The halfway covenant, I would maintain then, was neither a sign of decline in piety nor a betrayal of the standards of the founding fathers, but an honest attempt to rescue the concept of a church of visible saints from the tangle of problems created in time by human reproduction. Nevertheless, the halfway covenant does mark the end of a phase in Puritan church history during which ministers and church members were so dazzled by the pure new institution they had succeeded in creating that they were for the moment blinded to their obligations to the rest of New England and to the world. The halfway covenant, taken by itself, was a narrow tribal way of recruiting saints, for it wholly neglected the church's evangelical mission to perishing sinners outside the families of its members. But it did turn attention, in however limited a manner, to the problem of propagating the church. As Jonathan Mitchel said, in defending the synod of 1662, "The Lord hath not set up Churches onely that *a few old Christians* may keep one another warm while they live, and then carry away the Church into the cold grave with them when they dye: no, but that they might, with all the care, and with all the Obligations, and Advantages to that care that may be, *nurse up* still successively *another Generation* of Subjects to Christ that may stand up in his *Kingdome* when they are gone, that so he might have a People and Kingdome *successively* continued to him from one Generation to another." With the New England churches' recognition of this obligation, the Puritans' single-minded march toward purity came to rest.

The halfway covenant brought into the open the difficulties that had been lurking in the Puritan conception of church membership from the beginning. From the time when the first Separatists left the Church of England until the establishment in Massachusetts of tests for saving faith, that conception had developed toward making the visible church a closer and closer approximation of the invisible. With the halfway covenant the Puritans recognized that they had pushed their churches to the outer limits of visibility; and the history of the idea we have been tracing reached, if not a stop, at least a turning point.

The case against the theocratic interpretation has been made primarily in the form of studies of Puritan ideas. Younger historians such as DARRETT B. RUTMAN (1929-), professor of American history at the University of Minnesota, are turning to investigations of particular communities in order to explore fully the relationships between ideas and actions. As Rutman summarizes the results, they offer not only a fresh point of view on many of the classic problems of interpretation, but also induce a skepticism about the history of ideas approach to Puritanism. If his method is different, does Rutman actually reach conclusions about Puritan society and political life that are drastically at odds with the revisionist interpretation?*

Local Freedom and Puritan Control

"Puritanism" is a time-honored word in American history. On the highest level of scholarship it signifies a concept dear to historians who have made a life's work defining the New England "mind" and its role in the evolution of a peculiar American "mind." On the lowest level it is one of many catchwords and slogans which serve to half-educate our youth, a capsule description to distinguish the New England colonies from those to the south and explain the course of New England's institutional and political development. On either level, the historians' "Puritanism" would seem to be their own creation, a stereotype which, as any intimate view of a "Puritan" community will show, has little to do with reality in New England.

The stereotype has arisen as the result of a tendency among historians of early New England, and particularly the intellectual historians who have dominated the field in the last generation, to limit themselves to the study of the writings of the articulate few, on the assumption that the public professions of the ministers and magistrates constitute a true mirror of the New England mind. [1] The historian seeking to understand a New England concept of authority, for example, has familiarized

---

*From Darrett B. Rutman's essay, "The Mirror of Puritan Authority," in George A. Billias, ed., *Law and Authority in Colonial America: Selected Essays* (Barre, Mass.: Barre Publishing Company), © 1965. Reprinted with some footnotes omitted by permission of the author and Barre Publishing Company.

himself with the literature of England and Europe relative to the nature of man in society. He has scanned the works of such lay leaders of early New England as John Winthrop, noting his "little speech" on liberty of July 1645 and his earlier "A Modell of Christian Charity": "God Almightie in his most holy and wise providence hath soe disposed of the Condicion of mankinde, as in all times some must be rich some poore, some highe and eminent in power and dignitie; others meane and in subjeccion." He has thumbed through the ministerial writings to find Thomas Hooker: "However it is true, [that] the rule bindes such to the duties of their places and relations, yet it is certain, it requires that they should *first freely ingage* themselves in such covenants, and *then* be carefull to fullfill such duties." Or perhaps he has dipped into the pages of John Cotton: "It is evident by the light of nature, that all civill Relations are founded in Covenant. For, to passe by naturall Relations between Parents and Children, and Violent Relations, between Conquerors and Captives; there is no other way given whereby a people. . .can be united or combined into one visible body, to stand by mutuall Relations, fellow-members of the same body, but onely by mutuall Covenant; as appeareth between husband and wife in the family, Magistrates and subjects in the Commonwealth, fellow Citizens in the same Citie."

On occasion, the historian has turned also to the law, noting that it is replete with examples of the intrusion of authority into every aspect of New England life: "Taking into consideration the great neglect of many parents and masters in training up their children in learning, and labor, and other implyments which may be proffitable to the common wealth," it is ordered that the selectmen of every town "shall henceforth stand charged with the care of the redresse of this evill"; "forasmuch as in these countryes, where the churches of Christ are seated, the prosperity of the civil state is much advanced and blessed of God" and the ministers' preaching of the word "is of generall and common behoofe to all sorts of people, as being the ordinary meanes to subdue the harts of hearers not onely to the faith, and obedience to the Lord Jesus, but also to civill obedience, and allegiance unto magistracy" it is ordered that "every person shall duely resort and attend" to church services; it is ordered that "hereafter, noe dwelling howse shalbe builte above halfe a myle from the meeteing howse."

From such sources modern historians have drawn a picture of a highly cohesive and ordered social structure in which authority was omnipresent—the authority of the father in the family, of the minister in the church, of the magistrate in town and commonwealth. Both the cohesiveness of society and the authority were God-ordained, for man from the moment of Adam's fall was a degenerate being who required the oversight of his fellows in order to avoid the worst of sins. ("*In multitude of counsellers is safetie,*" Cotton was fond of saying.) Within the family, the father's authority was a natural concomitant to parenthood. But for the rest, man chose for himself. He submitted himself to the oversight of a congregation and through it a presbytery of ministers and elders, and to the civil authority of a king or prince or magistrate. Having sub-

[1] One takes "judicial notice" of the late Perry Miller's influence in molding our view of New England. See his *The New England Mind: From Colony to Province* (Cambridge, Mass., 1953), x: "As far as possible I have again employed the premise of my general title, that 'mind' means what was said and done publicly. Therefore I have made sparing use of diaries or private papers."

mitted, however, he was bound by a godly duty to "faithe patience, obedience." Thus the ministers wrote that the congregations were obliged to "yeeld obedience to their Overseers, in whatsoever they see and hear by them commanded to them from the Lord"; the magistrates that "we have our authority from God, in way of an ordinance, such as hath the image of God eminently stamped upon it, the contempt and violation whereof hath been vindicated with examples of divine vengeance." To further the interests of the community as a whole, the individual's personal aspirations were to be sublimated. "Goe forth, everyman that goeth, with a publicke spirit, looking not on your owne things onely, but also on the things of others," Cotton commanded the settlers who sailed with Winthrop in 1630. And Winthrop echoed him: "Wee must be knitt together in this worke as one man." Magistrates and ministers, too, were committed to the welfare of the entire community. The ministry was to guide the community in the way of God's truth. The civil authorities were to preserve the community in its liberty to do "that only which is good, just, and honest." The "ultimate and supreme" goal of both was that "the common Good of the Society, State or Kingdom" be preserved and "*God in all things. . .glorified.*"

The current view of New England Puritanism, of which this view of New England authority is but a part, rests upon two major implicit assumptions. The first is that there is such a thing as "Puritanism"—a term impossible perhaps to define, but capable nevertheless of being described—and that the acme of Puritan ideals is to be found in New England during the years 1630-1650. After that date, it is asserted, degeneration set in and there was a gradual falling away from the Puritan ideal. George L. Haskins, the outstanding writer on law and authority in early Massachusetts, reflects this assumption when he writes that "the initial decades of the Bay Colony's existence were the formative years" when, "under the pervasive influence of Puritan doctrine," government, law, ecclesiastical polity, and social structure were fully shaped; "the early social and political structure was to endure for several decades, but it gradually crumbled as primitive zeals began to wane and the religious aspects of life were subordinated to commercial interests."

Haskins owes an unacknowledged debt to Cotton Mather and other New England Jeremiahs, for the notion of Puritan quintessence and decline goes back to Mather's day. Sitting down to pen his *Magnalia Christi Americana* at the end of the seventeenth century, Mather was convinced that the years in which he was living were degenerate ones, that the years preceding his—the founding years—had constituted a golden age of which he was one of the few pure survivors. By telling the story of the past and its leaders he hoped to call his own time to the dutiful obedience to God's will (in both religious and social matters) which had previously prevailed. Mather's motive was succinctly set forth in the introduction to his sketches of the lives of the early ministers: "Reader, behold these *examples;* admire and follow what thou dost behold *exemplary* in them. They are offered unto the publick, with the intention. . .that *patterns* may have upon us the force which *precepts* have not."

This first assumption, though old, has proved of great pragmatic value to the modern historian. Having established that the first decades of New England were the acme of Puritanism, the historian can turn around and describe Puritanism in terms of what he has found in New England during those early years. Hence, he can avoid the problem of defining Puritanism, a task which Samuel Eliot Morison once found distasteful but necessary. The historian can also evade the issue of separating those facets of New England thought and character which were uniquely Puritan from those which merely reflected the way of life in England. Moreover, by accepting Mather's progression from golden age to degeneration, the historian can conceptualize Puritanism by drawing upon a vast quantity of material without worrying whether his sources are being used out of context as regards time, place, or persons. If Puritanism can "best be described as that point of view, that philosophy of life, that code of values, which was carried to New England by the first settlers in the early seventeenth century" and became "one of the continuous factors in American life and thought," as a leading anthology by Perry Miller and Thomas H. Johnson asserts, then certainly (the historian reasons) one can postulate a unique and unchanging Puritan ideal of society in terms of the letters and tracts emanating from New England during the first two decades of settlement, and, with increasing caution in view of the degeneration, from the whole of the seventeenth century. The same anthology contains selections from Winthrop's 1630 "Modell of Christian Charity" through John Wise's 1717 *Vindication of the Government of New-England Churches* to exemplify a Puritan theory of state and society, and concludes that:

> the most obvious lesson of the selections printed herein is that. . .the theorists of New England thought of society as a unit, bound together by inviolable ties; they thought of it not as an aggregation of individuals but as an organism, functioning for a definite purpose, with all parts subordinate to the whole, all members contributing a definite share, every person occupying a particular status. . . .The society of early New England was decidedly 'regimented.' Puritans did not think the state was merely an umpire, standing on the side lines of a contest, limited to checking egregious fouls, but otherwise allowing men free play according to their abilities and the breaks of the games. . . .The state to them was an active instrument of leadership, discipline, and, wherever necessary, of coercion. . . .The commanders were not to trim their policies by the desires of the people, but to drive ahead upon the predetermined course. . . .There was no questioning that men who would not serve the purposes of the society should be whipped into line. The objectives were clear and unmistakable; any one's disinclination to dedicate himself to them was obviously so much recalcitrancy and depravity.

The second major assumption is that one is free to ignore the "if" in Winthrop's "little speech" on liberty: "If you stand for your natural corrupt liberties, and will do what is good in your own eyes, you will not endure the least weight of authority, but will murmur, and oppose, and be always striving to shake off that yoke." Winthrop had, of course, no call to speak of those who "stand" for natural liberties unless there were individuals who took such a point of view. Similarly, one assumes oneself free to ignore the nature of the law—that law reflects not merely the assumptions of society, but the antithesis of those assumptions. The law calling upon town selectmen to insure the proper upbringing of children when their parents were neglecting to educate them to serve the community indicates not only that children were expected to receive such an education, but implies strongly that some children were *not* being prepared in the prescribed manner. The law requiring settlers to build their houses within a half-mile of the agencies of social control—church and magistrates—not only echoes the ideal of a cohesive society, but the fact that some persons were perfectly willing to break with the ideal and scatter across the rich New England countryside. One indication that the law (and the ideal it reflected) was being disregarded is a 1639 letter written by the Plymouth congregation to Boston's First Church "concerning the holding of Farmes of which there is noe lesse frequent use with your selves then with us. . .by means of [which] a mans famylie is Divided so in busie tymes they cannot (except upon the Lord's day) all of them joyne with him in famylie duties." The repeal of the Massachusetts law in 1640 on the grounds that it was unenforceable is still further substantiation.

The assumption is not without its rationalization. If the historian accepts as a matter of faith that, as Richard Schlatter writes, "it was the Puritan leaders who shaped the culture of New England, whatever the rank and file may have wanted"—an extension of the notion of a Puritan oligarchy from the political to the social milieu—then it is easy to explain away those who disregarded the law or who stood for "natural corrupt liberties." Once again, Mather has provided the modern historian with a readymade answer. To him incidents of social and religious dissent were merely the "continual *temptation* of the devil" which were, at least in the early years, overcome by the pure in heart.

That an ideal arrangement of society was visualized by some of the first comers to New England and that they contemplated realizing the ideal in the New World is patently obvious. One need only glance at Winthrop's "Modell of Christian Charity" to see it. But was the ideal uniquely Puritan? The thought that men, like the diverse parts of nature, ideally stood in ordered symmetry is to be found in Shakespeare's *Troilus and Cressida*:

> The heavens themselves, the planets and this centre,
> Observe degree, priority and place.
> . . .O, when degree is shaked,
> Which is the ladder of all high designs,
> The enterprise is sick! How could communities . . .
> Prerogative of age, crowns, sceptres, laurels,
> But by degree, stand in authentic place?

The notion of men entering society by compact or covenant and thereby binding themselves to authority was a pervading theme in Western thought, although particularly relevant for the religious polemicists of the sixteenth and seventeenth centuries. One finds it, for example, in the *Vindiciae Contra Tyrannos* of the French Protestants and in Richard Hooker's *Ecclesiastical Polity*. In Hooker's work, too, is found the idea of the divine nature of authority once established by man: "God creating mankind did endue it naturally with full power to guide itself, in what kind of societies soever it should choose to live," yet those on whom power "is bestowed even at men's discretion, they likewise do hold it by divine right" for "albeit God do neither appoint the thing nor assign the person; nevertheless when men have established both, who doth doubt that sundry duties and offices depending thereupon are prescribed in the word of God"; therefore, "we by the law of God stand bound meekly to acknowledge them for God's lieutenants."

More importantly, was the ideal—so often expressed by the articulate few and commented upon by the intellectual historians—ever a reality in New England? Certainly conditions in America were not conducive to it. The very ideal contained a flaw, for while in England the social and religious covenant was an abstract principle to be toyed with by logicians, in New England it was, in town and church, transformed into practice. How does one convince the generality that the forms and personnel of authority are within its province, but that once established they are in God's domain and are to be honored as such? What spokesman for New England orthodoxy could surpass Ireland's Cuchulinn in battling the waves of the sea? Moreover, the transition from old to New England constituted a break in the social fabric familiar to the individual. In an English borough or village the individual located himself according to well-established social and political relationships, but these were no more. Family ties in New England during the early years were relatively few. Ties to the traditional elements of authority—vestrymen, churchwardens, manor stewards, borough councillors, justices-of-the-peace—had disappeared, to be created anew in the New England town, it is true, but such new relationships lacked the sanctity of long familiarity. And even when new ties existed, there was little stability in the New Englander's place in the social and political order. What mattered the regular assertion that God had ordained some to ride and some to walk when those who walked one day could, by virtue of the absence of traditional leaders, the presence of New World opportunities, and the application of their own diligence, ride another?

Such musings give a hint of the answer as to whether the ideal was ever a reality in New England. For more than a hint, however, one must turn to the New Englander's own habitat, his town. For many historians such research necessitates a shift to an entirely different set of sources. It means leaving behind published sermons, tracts, and laws and turning instead to town and church records. It calls for an end to the relatively comfortable perusal of the writings of a few and undertaking the drudgery of culling local records to identify the persons in a given town—their backgrounds, landholdings, economic activities, social and economic affiliations, and politics. Research of such nature is time-consuming, but the rewards are rich.

One such study is that of Sudbury, Massachusetts, undertaken by Sumner Chilton Powell. Sudbury was a small interior town devoted to the raising of cattle. It was not directly affected by the turn of trade and commerce in the 1640s as were some other communities. Moreover, its population was relatively homogeneous during the period with which Powell dealt. One might expect, therefore, that all the generalizations respecting Puritan attitudes would be reflected in the activities of Sudbury's people. But Powell's story is far from that. The founders were acquisitive English yeomen, little touched by any formal Puritan movement in England. During the town's first years, its people were devoted to building and cultivating the land, using the "open-field" or common agricultural method which most of them had known in England. In the early 1650s, however, they felt the pinch of too little land and solicited the General Court for an additional tract. The subsequent enlargement opened Pandora's box. One segment of the town demanded a shift to closed agriculture—large tracts individually operated—and a division by which "every man shall enjoy a like quantity of land"; another resisted. This issue became entangled with a second, the desire of some to build a new meeting house. Matters were complicated still further by a third issue, the desire of the older settlers to limit the number of cattle allowed on the town meadow. The heated debates that followed involved every person in the town, including minister Edmund Brown. Town meetings became "exciting and well-attended"; tempers flared. In the end, the town split, one faction moving away to found Marlborough, Massachusetts.

The debates divided the town into warring factions, Peter Noyes and Edmund Goodnow representing the first settlers and heads of families, John Ruddock and John How leading the younger men of the town, and minister Brown acting largely in his own interest. At one point Goodnow declared that, "be it right or wrong, we will have [our way]. . .if we can have it no other way, we will have it by club law." At another point, How threatened secession by the young men: "If you oppresse the poore, they will cry out; and if you persecute us in one city, wee must fly to another." Pastor Brown called a meeting "to see to the constraining of youth from the profanation of the Lord's day in time of public service" and turned the session into a political harangue; subsequently the minister appeared at a town meeting to cry out he would "put it to a Vote, before I would be nosed by them." Townsmen refused to attend Sabbath lectures and services for fear of being "ensnared" by their political opponents. One party visited the minister "to desire him not to meddle" and Ruddock bluntly told his pastor that, "setting aside your office, I regard you no more than another man." The Reverend Mr. Brown ultimately attempted to have the dispute submitted to a council of elders drawn from neighboring churches, but the various factions refused on the grounds that "it was a civil difference." Where in this debate is there any indication that the New Englanders "thought of society as a unit, bound together by inviolable ties. . .all parts subordinate to the whole. . .every person occupying a particular status"?

In Boston, too, much the same story is to be found: actions quite contrary to attitudes so often generalized upon. In 1634, the generality—again, a relatively homogeneous populace—challenged the town's leadership by demanding an immediate division of all available land on an equal basis. The response of the leadership was to some extent based on attitudes made classic by historians. Winthrop, thinking in terms of the community, argued against the allocation of more land than an individual could use, partly out of his desire "to prevent the neglect of trades, and other more necessary employments" and "partly that there might be place to receive such as should come after." To him, it would be "very prejudicial" if newcomers "should be forced to go far off for land, while others had much, and could make no use of it, more than to please their eye with it." But the townsmen would have none of it. Land was too much a way to personal gain.

The issue reached a climax in December when a committee of seven was elected to divide the town lands. Winthrop "and other of the chief men" failed of election. The townsmen feared "that the richer men would give the poorer sort no great proportions of land" and chose "one of the elders and a deacon, and the rest of the inferior sort." All the advocates of an ordered society were brought to bear to overturn the election. Winthrop spoke of his grief "that Boston should be the first who should shake off their magistrates," and the Reverend Mr. Cotton of "the Lord's order among the Israelites" by which "all such businesses" were "committed to the elders." "It had been nearer the rule," Cotton argued, "to have chosen some of each sort." The generality gave way for the moment and agreed to a new election. Subsequently a more proper committee was chosen "to devide and dispose" of the land "leaving such portions in Common for the use of newe Commers, and the further benefitt of the towne, as in theire best discretions they shall thinke fitt."

The battle, however, was by no means over. The pursuit of individual gain continued to prompt political activity. The prevailing economic view (and one not uniquely Puritan) was that all phases of the economy were subject to government regulation. Town governments in Massachusetts had the authority to regulate land distribution, land usage, and the laying out of streets; in Boston, the town government established embryonic building codes and licensed inns and wharves. Given this actual exercise of power over the various avenues of opportunity, it was to one's advantage to participate in public affairs.

Land, for a time, continued to be the principal issue. The town had a limited area into which it could expand. By the second decade it had become difficult to find plots for newcomers or additional acreage for older settlers. In 1641, popular pressure forced the selectmen to review the larger grants made in the 1630s, but this action served little purpose. Even where surveys indicated that a Winthrop, Oliver or Cotton held more land than had been allocated, the selectmen took no remedial action. During the following year, the selectmen—in order to obtain more room on Boston's tiny peninsula for house lots—resurrected an earlier order denying the inhabitants permanent possession of their lots in the Boston fields. The result was an angry town meeting in which the order was repealed "for peace sake, and for avoyding of confusion in the Towne."

Boston's turn to trade in the 1640s brought about a change. Opportunities for personal aggrandizement in land were gradually replaced by the better chances for advancement in commerce and allied crafts such as coopering, leatherworking, and shipbuilding. For the artisan, participation in local government was equally as important as it had been for those persons interested in land. The leatherworker or butcher, subject to the selectmen under local regulations regarding the cleanliness of his establishment, or even his very right to carry on his trade within the town, of necessity participated in the town meetings to elect the men who could, in a moment, curtail or end his business activities. The retailer, subject to the inspection of clerks of the market operating under commonwealth law, was quick to make known his choice for such officials. Almost everyone engaged in any kind of economic activity—the laws limiting the electorate notwithstanding—sought to vote for the deputies to the General Court and the Assistants inasmuch as these men wrote the commonwealth ordinances governing economic activity.

On the inter-town level in Massachusetts, too, the desire for personal aggrandizement played havoc with the ideal of an orderly and cohesive society. Town rivalries arose; boundary disputes raged interminably between communities, the prize being a rich meadow or copse. Craftsmen in one town were jealous of those in another. Shoemakers outside Boston, for example, objected to shoemakers within that town organizing a company and seeking exclusive privileges regarding shoes sold in the Boston market. Do not allow "our Brethren of Boston" to "have power put into their hands to hinder a free trade," they wrote to the General Court. "Keeping out Country shoomakers from Coming into the Market," they continued, "wil weaken the hands of the Country shoomakers from using their trade, or occasion them to Remove to Boston which wilbe hurtful to Other townes." Merchants and tradesmen in the northern towns—Ipswich, Salem, Newbury—bitterly resented the fact that

"Boston, being the chiefest place of resort of Shipping, carries away all the Trade." They reacted in a series of political moves aimed at reducing Boston's central position in the commonwealth. An effort was made to move the seat of government from Boston; an attempt got underway to change the basis of representation in the House of Deputies to Boston's disadvantage; and an alliance was formed between northern towns and country towns to create a bloc within the House to oppose those towns immediately around Boston harbor.

The political activity in and among the towns suggests that the people of Massachusetts Bay, and one can extrapolate to include the other New England colonies, were not acting within the concept of authority and cohesive, ordered society which modern historians have so carefully delineated and pronounced to be characteristic of Puritanism and Puritan New England. Society was not something to which the people of the Bay commonwealth invariably subordinated their own interests. Indeed, the abstract concept of "society" seems to have held little meaning for a generality intent upon individual pursuits. Nor was authority a pervasive thing, obliging the individual through family, church, and state to sublimate his personal aspirations to the interests of the community as a whole. The "state" in Sudbury—in the form of either town or commonwealth government—could provide no other solution to the town's disputes than to permit the community to divide. The church—the Reverend Mr. Brown personally and the elders of the neighboring churches invited in by Brown—was unable to interpose its authority to settle matters. Family fidelity failed to check the personal aspirations of the "landless young sons" who followed Ruddock and How.

The people of Massachusetts, it would appear, were coming to view the elements of authority as being divided rather than united. In particular, they viewed the church and state as distinct entities with well-defined (and to a large extent mutually exclusive) areas of operation. In Sudbury, for example, Pastor Brown's intervention in a civil affair led to his being asked not to "meddle." In Boston, the calling of the Synod of 1646-48 by the commonwealth government roused strong opposition from those who lashed out against the interjection of "civil authority" in church business. The conflict so begun would eventuate in a full scale assault upon the imposition of ministerial authority within the church and of synodical authority among churches—further evidence that the historians' concept of authority and cohesiveness bears little resemblance to New England reality. The historians might cite as evidence of the concept the Cambridge *Platform* which emanated from the Synod and pronounced ministerial and synodical authority to be part of the New England Way, but the deathbed utterances of the Reverend John Wilson are more to the point. Wilson cited as "those sins amongst us, which provoked the displeasure of God" the rising up of the people "*against their Ministers. . .when indeed they do but Rule for Christ,*" and "*the making light of, and not subjecting to the Authority of* Synods, *without which the Churches cannot long subsist.*"

The same dichotomy between church and state which one finds in the towns may be seen on the commonwealth level. The historians have noted all too often those laws passed by civil authorities to further the views of the church and those cases where the ministry advised the magistrates on civil matters. But they have paid far too little attention to the arduous efforts made to define the respective spheres of church and state. As John Cotton wrote in 1640, "the government of the Church is as the Kingdome of Christ is, not of this world, but spirituall and heavenly. . . . The power of the keyes is far distant from the power of the sword." To him church and state in Massachusetts were involved in the same task, "the Establishment of pure Religion, in doctrine, worship, and [church] government, according to the word of God: As also the reformation of all corruptions in any of these." Hence the ministers, in whose care the word of God was placed, could logically press for "sweet and wholsom" laws and "civil punishments upon the willfull opposers and disturbers" of the church. But for the things of this world—"the disposing of mens goods or lands, lives or liberties, tributes, customes, worldly honors, and inheritances"—"in these the Church submitteth, and refereth it self to the civill state."

For the most part, too, historians in the past few years have tended to overlook those cases where there was a clash between magistrates and ministers. In 1639, the General Court decided that too frequent and overly long church meetings were detrimental to the community and asked the elders "to consider about the length and frequency of church assemblies." The ministers promptly denounced the magistrates. The request "cast a blemish upon the elders," they said, one "which would remain to posterity, that they should need to be regulated by the civil magistrates." The over-anxious intervention of an elder in a matter before the Assistants in 1643, on the other hand, drove one magistrate to exasperation. "Do you think to come with your eldership here to carry matters?" he shouted. On another occasion, when the elders of Essex County went beyond the bounds that Winthrop considered proper in espousing the cause of the northern towns against Boston—for when town argued with town the elders tended to identify with their communities—the governor lashed out. They "had done no good offices in this matter, through their misapprehensions both of the intentions of the magistrates, and also of the matters themselves, being affairs of state, which did not belong to their calling."

In the division of authority that was taking place, it would seem that the church was freely conceded the power of opening and closing the doors of heaven. To whatever extent the individual sought heaven, he honored the authority of the church in moral and theological matters. But the keys to personal aggrandizement in this world were lodged with the state, and the generality was coming to look upon the state in a peculiarly modern way. In one sense the state was the servant of the individual, obligated to foster his welfare and prosperity. At the same time, it was to protect him from the aspirations of others—acting, so to speak, as an umpire for society, exercising authority in such a way as to avoid collisions between members of the community who were following their individual yet concentric orbits. One can perceive such a view of society, however obliquely, in the political theory of the later New Englanders. For indeed, their writings on this matter are not all of a piece. There is a subtle difference between a Winthrop or Cotton for whom the goal of society was the pleasing of God; a Samuel Willard to whom a happy, contented people was most pleasing to God; and a John Wise to whom "the Happiness of the People, is the End of its [the state's] Being; or main Business to be attended and done."

The view of society discernible in the New England community is quite different from that expounded by intellectual historians who have turned to the writings of the articulate few—and little else—as their mirror of New England's mind. Are we to discard their mirror and the "Puritan" concepts which they have seen in it? The purpose of intellectual history is to delineate the ideological framework within which a people acted. If the actions of the people under consideration do not fall within the framework created, it follows that the framework is invalid. It is not that simple, of course. In the case of New England, the intellectual framework erected over the past years has been firmly based upon the writings of the leading laymen and clergy in the society. We must accept such works as a valid expression of their ideals, even though their ideals might not apply to the people as a whole.

But what are we to describe as "Puritan," the ideals of the articulate few which, relative to society and authority, were neither unique nor pervasive, or the actuality of the man in the street—more accurately, the man in the village lane—which does not fit the ideals? The very fact that such a question can be asked would seem to imply that the description of New England in terms of Puritanism, or of Puritanism in terms of New England, is erroneous. Certainly, the concept of a Puritan golden age, followed by decline, disappears. Mather's degeneration is, in large part, nothing more than the insistence by the generality upon a relationship between the individual and society rather different from that held to by the leaders. And the golden age, as Mather himself admitted, was marked by continual controversies which "made neighbours that should have been like *sheep*, to 'bite and devour one another' " and inspired "unaccountable *party-making*," a symptom of that different relationship.

The historian must, of course, address himself to the problem of New England's intellectuals. Isolated from reality as they were, they clung for almost half a century to ideals which grew more outdated with the passing of each day, and then gradually and subtly accomodated their ideals to the realities of the situation facing them. But their accomodation and the forces in society that caused them to make changes represent a much more important aspect of history than the mere description of "Puritanism." And the historian must dispense with the easy generalization that such leaders "shaped" New England's culture regardless of what "the rank and file may have wanted." He must seek instead to understand the rank and file, their motivations, aspirations, and achievements. For in the last analysis which is more vital, an ideological "Puritanism" divorced from reality which has received so much attention over the years, or the reality which has received so little attention but which was in essence laying down the basis for two-and-a-half centuries of American history ahead?

Suggestions for Additional Reading

The bibliography that follows is selective. Hundreds of other books and articles on New England Puritanism are listed at the end of *The Puritans, A Sourcebook of Their Writings* (New York, 1938), edited by Perry Miller and Thomas H. Johnson. In the paperback edition of this book (2 vols; New York, 1963) the bibliography is carried up through 1962; it includes references to writings by the Puritans themselves, as well as to works about Puritanism. Many of the titles are briefly described. Another useful source of information is the bibliographical volume of the *Literary History of the United States* (New York, 1948), edited by Robert Spiller *et. al.* A *Bibliography Supplement* (New York, 1959) edited by Richard M. Ludwig, extends the coverage of Spiller through 1957.

No interpretation can match the vigor and excitement of the Puritans' own writings. Fortunately a number of these are available in modern editions. Perhaps the most celebrated book by an American Puritan is William Bradford's *Of Plymouth Plantation*, a moving narrative about the Pilgrims who founded Plymouth Colony in 1620. Of the many editions, the most useful and accurate is that edited by Samuel E. Morison (New York, 1952). For Massachusetts, the *Journal*, or *History of New England* by John Winthrop (2 vols; New York, 1953) is an unparalleled source of information about life in the colony; it is equally revealing of Winthrop himself. Finally there is Cotton Mather's *Magnalia Christi Americana* (2 vols; Hartford, Conn., 1853-1855). The *Magnalia* was the first comprehensive history of Massachusetts, written in the 1690s when the Holy Commonwealth was fast breaking up, but it falls into the category of an original source by reason of Mather's proximity to the events and attitudes he describes.

The anthology of Miller and Johnson's contains selections from these three books and many more. The texts are selected and arranged to agree with the interpretation of the revisionists. A generous selection of Puritan poetry reminds readers of the Puritans' devotion to the literary arts; a section on "Manners, Customs, and Behavior" dispells the picture of gloomy inhibitions painted by earlier historians. The theological texts document the transition from the covenant theology of the seventeenth century to the rationalism of the eighteenth; those on political thought, the development of modern conceptions of liberty and government out of the social covenant. Merely by making the Puritans' own words so easily available, *The Puritans* became an effective means of counteracting the theocratic interpretation.

But the attack upon that interpretation began more than a decade earlier when Kenneth Murdock, a professor of English at Harvard, published a biography of *Increase Mather, the Foremost American Puritan* (Cambridge, Mass., 1925). By vindicating Mather of many of the charges against him, Murdock contributes significantly to the reappraisal of the Puritans. Within the next fifteen years the two leading revisionist historians, Samuel Eliot Morison and Perry Miller, published their major works. Morison began with *Builders of the Bay Colony* (Boston, 1930), a book that is still the best introduction to Massachusetts life and history. Then he wrote a three-volume history of Harvard College, *The Founding of Harvard College; Harvard College in the Seventeenth Century* (Cambridge, Mass., 1935-1936). In *The Puritan Pronaos* (New York, 1936), reprinted in paperback as *The Intellectual Life of Colonial New England*), Morison sketched other aspects of educational and intellectual life in New England.

Perry Miller, in addition to editing *The Puritans,* wrote *Orthodoxy in Massachusetts* (Cambridge, Mass., 1933) and *The New England Mind: The Seventeenth Century* (New York, 1939; reprinted Cambridge, Mass., 1954). The proper order in which to read them, as he explained later, is to begin with *The New England Mind,* which describes that "mind" as though it were a closed system of ideas. The rise of certain of these ideas in Elizabethan England and the gradual disintegration of the "mind" in New England can be traced in *Orthodoxy in Massachusetts* (which deals primarily with the history of Congregationalism) and *The New England Mind: From Colony to Province* (Cambridge, Mass., 1953), which carries the story of change from the 1640s to 1730. Besides these volumes, Miller wrote many important essays on Puritanism, some of which—including his most famous article, "The Marrow of Puritan Divinity"—are collected in *Errand into the Wilderness* (Cambridge, Mass., 1956).

Morison and Miller were joined by some of their students in the growing reaction to the theocratic interpretation. Clifford K. Shipton spoke out in a number of articles: "A Plea for Puritanism," *American Historical Review,* LX (1935), 460-467; "Puritanism and Modern Democracy," *New England Historical and Genealogical Register,* CI (1947), 181-198; and "The New England Clergy in the 'Glacial Age,'" *Publications* of the Colonial Society of Massachusetts XXXI (1933), 24-54, this last a direct reply to Charles Francis Adams. Edmund Morgan turned to social history in *The Puritan Family* (Boston, 1944; revised edition, 1966), which re-examines the Puritans' attitude toward sex, among other things.

The picture of Puritanism these historians were attacking came from several books. The earliest were those by Charles F. and Brooks Adams. *The Emancipation of Massachusetts,* by Brooks, was published in 1887. Charles F. Adams's contributions were extensive: *Three Episodes of Massachusetts History* (2 vols; Boston, 1892); *History of Braintree, Massachusetts* (Cambridge, Mass., 1891); and a direct assault upon the filiopietism then characteristic of histories about New England, *Massachusetts, Its History and Its Historians* (Boston, 1891). In the 1920s the theocratic interpretation was put forth most persuasively in two books, *The Founding of New England* (Boston, 1921) by James Truslow Adams and *Main Currents in American Thought: The Colonial Mind* (New York, 1927) by Vernon Louis Parrington. Adams's book is still a convenient summary of the early history of New England. The theocratic point of view continues to have its exponents, as in Thomas J. Wertenbaker, *The Puritan Oligarchy* (New York, 1947) and A. L. Rowse, *The Elizabethans and America* (New York, 1959).

The older filiopietists are rarely read today, though some of their books are still useful. On the crudest level, this attitude toward Puritanism appears in the Mayflower Society orations delivered annually to commemorate the landing of the Pilgrims. The longest and in many ways most informative history of New England remains John Gorham Palfrey's *A Compendious History of New England* (5 vols; Boston, 1858-1890). Similarly, the most substantial descriptions of Congregationalism and church practices during the seventeenth century are works produced in the nineteenth century: Henry Martyn Dexter, *The Congregationalism of The Last Three Hundred Years* (New York, 1880); and Williston Walker, *The Creeds and Platforms of Congregationalism* (New York, 1893) and *A History of the Congregational Churches in the United States* (New York, 1894). Charles W. Upham, *Salem Witchcraft; with an Account of Salem Village* (2 vols; Boston, 1867; reprinted, New York, 1966) is an extraordinarily suggestive interpretation of the witchcraft episode.

On certain points the revisionist historians have been challenged. Professor Morison's interpretation of Harvard College is attacked by Winthrop S. Hudson in "The Morison Myth Concerning the Founding of Harvard College," *Church History,* VIII (1939), 148-159. Among the most debated issues in New England historiography is the origins of Congregationalism. The thesis that Miller set forth in *Orthodoxy in Massachusetts* has been modified or rejected by several more recent writers: Larzer Ziff, "The Salem Puritans in the

Free Aire of a New World," *Huntington Library Quarterly*, XX (1957), 373-384, and also in his biography of John Cotton, *The Career of John Cotton* (Princeton, N.J., 1962); Edmund S. Morgan, *Visible Saints* (New York, 1963); and Darrett B. Rutman, *Winthrop's Boston* (Chapel Hill, N.C., 1965). Others have challenged the significance of the "covenant" theology: Leonard J. Trinterud, "The Origins of Puritanism," *Church History*, XX (1951), 37-57; Everett H. Emerson, "Calvin and Covenant Theology," *Church History*, XXV (1956), 136-144; Jens Moller, "The Beginnings of Puritan Covenant Theology," *The Journal of Ecclesiastical History*, XIV (1963), 46-67; and Norman Pettit, *The Heart Prepared* (New Haven, Conn., 1966).

A different perspective on many of the problems about Puritanism in New England is provided in studies of Puritanism in England. Of the many excellent studies on English Puritanism, only a few are listed here. Marshall Knappen, *Tudor Puritanism* (Chicago, 1939) covers the sixteenth century. William Haller, *The Rise of Puritanism* (New York, 1938), brings the story to the 1630s, and is the best introduction to the subject. Geoffrey Nuttall, *The Holy Spirit in Puritan Faith and Experience* (Oxford, England, 1946), is an important study of a key theological issue among radical Puritans. Nuttall has also written a study of Congregationalism as it developed in England, *Visible Saints: The Congregational Way, 1640-1660* (Oxford, England, 1957), which should be compared (but not confused) with E. S. Morgan's book of the same title. The broader religious background of Puritanism is described in John T. McNeill, *The History and Character of Calvinism* (New York, 1954). In *The Protestant Mind of the English Reformation* (Princeton, N.J., 1961), Charles and Katherine George challenge many of the traditional conceptions about English Puritanism; they are replied to in John F. H. New, *Anglican and Puritan* (Palo Alto, Calif., 1964). Alan Simpson is explicitly comparative in *Puritanism in Old and New England* (Chicago, 1955).

From the background of their English heritage came many of the colonists' ideas about society, education, and politics. Wallace Notestein's survey of English life and institutions, *The English People on the Eve of Colonization* (New York, 1954), is extremely useful for this reason. It is important to know why the Puritans left England, since their motives for leaving affected their behavior in the colonies. These motives are debated in Allen French, *Charles I and the Puritan Upheaval* (Boston, 1957); Nellis M. Crouse, "Causes of the Great Migration 1630-1640," *New England Quarterly*, V (1932), 3-36, a reply to James Truslow Adams's economic interpretation; and Perry Miller, "Errand into the Wilderness," *Errand into the Wilderness* (Cambridge, Mass., 1956). The constitutional and political development of each of the New England colonies is described in Charles M. Andrews, *The Colonial Background of American History*, volumes I and II (New Haven, Conn., 1934-1936).

The political development of Massachusetts has been studied from many points of view. The focus for debate is the figure of John Winthrop and the political evolution of Massachusetts during the first two decades. Edmund S. Morgan's short biography of John Winthrop, *The Puritan Dilemma* (Boston, 1958) should be compared with James Truslow Adams's interpretation in *The Founding of New England* and the sketch by Morison in *Builders of the Bay Colony*. Perry Miller attacks Parrington's point of view in an early essay, "Thomas Hooker and the Democracy of Connecticut," included in *Errand into the Wilderness*. The role that Roger Williams played during these years is debated in Samuel H. Brockunier, *The Irrepressible Democrat, Roger Williams* (New York, 1940); Perry Miller, *Roger Williams, His Contribution to the American Tradition* (Indianapolis, Ind., 1953); Alan Simpson, "How Democratic Was Roger Williams?" *William and Mary Quarterly*, 3d series, XIII (1956), 56-67; and Edmund S. Morgan, "Miller's Williams," *New England Quarterly* XXXVIII (1965), 513-523. B. Katherine Brown disagrees with James Truslow Adams on the number of voters in Massachusetts in "Freemanship in Massachusetts," *American Historical Review*, LIX (1954), 865-883. Ellen Brennan, "The Massachusetts Council of the Magistrates," *New England Quarterly* IV (1931), 54-93, traces the history of a special political issue. The development of a law code is thoroughly studied in George Lee Haskins, *Law and Authority in Early Massachusetts* (New York, 1960). And the Antinomian controversy, which had many political overtones, is analyzed by Emery Battis, *Saints and Sectaries* (Chapel Hill, N.C., 1963).

As society in New England evolved, it broke away from patterns of English life and created new patterns that were distinctively "American." Two of the best analyses of social change have come through detailed investigations of a single community: Boston, in Darrett B. Rutman, *Winthrop's Boston* (Chapel Hill, N.C., 1965), and Sudbury, in Sumner C. Powell, *Puritan Village* (Middletown, Conn., 1963). Social and economic history are combined in Bernard Bailyn, *The New England Merchants in the Seventeenth Century* (Cambridge, Mass., 1955). Bailyn considers the question of social change more broadly in *Education in the Forming of American Society* (Chapel Hill, N.C., 1960), a book that is largely focused on the American family. Even the church has had its social historian: Ola Winslow, *Meetinghouse Hill* (New York, 1952).

For the cultural history of New England in the seventeenth century, there are surveys by Louis B. Wright, *The Cultural Life of the American Colonies* (New York, 1957) and Samuel E. Morison, *The Puritan Pronaos* (New York, 1935). Thomas G. Wright covers specifically *Literary Culture in Early New England* (New Haven, Conn., 1920), as does Kenneth B. Murdock, *Literature and Theology in Colonial New England* (Cambridge, Mass., 1949). Also useful is Harold S. Jantz, *The First Century of New England Verse* (Worcester, Mass., 1945).